THE ROMANCE
OF SHELLS

IN NATURE AND ART

THE ROMANCE
OF SHELLS

IN NATURE AND ART

by Louise Allderdice Travers

AVENEL BOOKS • NEW YORK

To my
encouraging and
extraordinarily patient
family and friends

ACKNOWLEDGMENTS

I am conscious of receiving inspiration and help from so many, among them my patient family and friends to whom I have dedicated this book. I would like to express particular gratitude also to:

Rachel L. Carson, beautiful writer and philosopher, for her books, and for reading mine and graciously commenting on it; and to Henry Laughlin of the Riverside Press for introducing me to her.

The New York Shell Club and the editors of its news letter, M. K. Jacobson and Dorothy Raeihle, and its illustrator, Anthony d'Attilio.

Dr. William K. Emerson, chairman of the Department of Living Invertebrates of the American Museum of Natural History, New York City, and, by his side, William E. Old, Museum Specialist, for their assistance in the identification of the shells used in my pictures here reproduced.

Maginel Wright Barney, who, through Ben Raeburn of the Horizon Press, found for me the quotation from a lecture by Frank Lloyd Wright, her brother, expressing his beautiful feeling for shells.

Elsie M. Dominguez, who graciously and generously has been so helpful with her gift, typing.

F. W. Bronson for snapping my granddaughter Ellen with me on his beach.

C. D. McArthur and Frederick Braun who first charmed me into buying shells.

5

Laura Franklin Delano for her lovely shell doorway on Sutton Place, so appropriate to illustrate my text.

Hans Van Nes for the color photographs of my pictures and of early pieces in my collection.

Betsy Allderdice Mudge for her drawing of the nautilus.

Rebekah Howard Collins, who created all the other drawings for this book with boundless enthusiasm and understanding; my debt to her is especially large.

L.A.T.

CONTENTS

LIST OF COLOR PLATES

1

Sailors' Valentines

Had anyone told me that a tiny white shell with black stripes—commonly called the zebra—would literally change my entire outlook and bring me untold happiness, too, I never would have believed him. But miracles, as we like to call such experiences, can happen for you and me.

It has always seemed to me that a woman's life is spent within three or four circles. Each circle, held by a mystical but firm band, confines certain periods of her life. The first one holds her childhood and is not too much her own to mold. Next comes that frantic phase when, even though she herself may not be conscious of it, she is figuratively running in circles to find a mate. This finally achieved, "for better or for worse," she moves into that larger sphere of home-making and family life, a woman's greatest joy and opportunity. This one is filled with love, the satisfaction of sacrificing and sharing, of disappointments and achievements, and of being leaned on. Thus the wife and mother.

Then, sometimes very quickly, this circle empties. Children seem to leave it all at the same moment. Statistics, plus our own observation of our friends, show us that a woman is often widowed at this same period.

That was my pattern.

So she moves on, then, into yet another circle. But it seems the encircling band has burst; it no longer seems confining but vast and void, much like a man's retiring. I have always felt fortunate that I needed more income and therefore knew I must work. This gave me a start for the first years. But as time went on—and woman's life-span is reported to be ever lengthening—it seemed that I must face an even longer and lonelier existence than I had thought. I prayed that something would come along, an interest that would prove truly absorbing yet not too hard work for a woman of my age.

In this period, of course, we find our children and grandchildren a great joy; but I for one didn't want to get in their hair too often. I wanted only to be helpful when needed. A wise pediatrician once said to me, "Of course, help when you're needed; but be a grandmother hard to find."

It did amuse me—a hiding grandmother! And what does a grandmother do in hiding? But this doctor backed up his advice with sound reasons gained from his experience with many families. It's such a temptation to advise, and hard indeed to let go of the ones you once possessed, even though you realize that they, perhaps, are wiser than you once were and that times have changed.

Well, to get back to that little zebra shell. It happened this way. Years ago, in an antique shop, I bought a double, octagonal wooden box, hinged so that it could be opened and closed. The inside of each half was filled with a solid mosaic pattern in shells. One half had a heart made of pink shells in its center; the other half, a rose made of shells. Then, worked in with some very dark shells, were the words "To My Sister." The remaining spaces were filled in with a design of brighter shells and the little striped snail shells.

Some years later, one of my daughters was going to be married and, as the box had cost just thirteen dollars (always my lucky number), I decided it was the perfect gift for her sister to give the bride. This meant, of course, that it left my home. From then on I was continually on the lookout for another one for myself. I had learned that it was called a "sailor's valentine" and tried, without success, to describe it to my antique-loving friends. It was years before I found a second one and, although the price had risen, I managed to have it. Since then I have acquired several more—they fascinate me both for their beauty and for the aura of romance that surrounds them.

There are two schools of thought as to their origin. I enjoyed the first of these which most stirs the imagination. I liked to think of young men and old sailing the seven seas. As they waited for wind and tide, they went gathering shells, exotic shells very different from those they had known on the beaches of Cape Cod, or their foggy English shores, for the warm tropical waters tend to produce gayer colors. The ship's carpenter would gladly make octagonal boxes for them, as he did in those days for sextant and compass. With long days to be passed on deck, these seamen arranged the shells in patterns to their liking for the women of their hearts who would never see the tropics or the Far East.

Although this was a lovely idea, as I found more valentines and did some research on them, I decided that they were made by the natives of Barbados. There is a similarity in the designs of these boxes to suggest a single source; and the paper linings are much alike. Barbados was the last port of call for whalers homeward bound. I'm inclined to believe that these men wouldn't have thought very much of gathering shells for females left at home while they themselves were basking in the sunshine and smiles of a very different life. But as they neared home, they would remember not to return empty-handed. The enterprising natives learned to solve the problems of these anxious shoppers by having valentines ready for them to buy on the last leg of their journey. There were varying sentiments—"Remember Me," "Love the Giver," "Welcome Home," "Gift to Mother," and "Gift from Barbados"—to take to their womenfolk waiting in New Bedford or Nantucket, or the more distant English ports. A friend of mine who is clever with her hands has repaired some of these valentines and found a newspaper, *The Barbadian*, May 15, 1833, used for backing. Some may have been made even earlier. She has one with the label of a Barbados dealer that reads: "Native Manufacturers in Fancy Work."

You have gleaned by now that I am one to haunt secondhand shops. I had paid a quarter, years before at a church rummage sale, for a candy box full of shells. I just couldn't resist shells—or is it a bargain I can't pass up? Gazing at my precious valentines one idle day, I thought, why can't I try making something with shells? Of course I didn't have an octagon box but, necessity being the mother of invention, items appeared from shelf and drawer—an old frame and the candy box and so on. These shells were rather nondescript, grey or beige clamlike shells, yellow jingle shells, and blue mussels. But one, though not even half an inch in size, did have a pattern. It was a white shell with varying black stripes following its contour. Like a zebra, I thought. How could it be so made? This was the one that lured me on.

I worked with tense excitement for several afternoons and I finally had a flower arrangement of shells in an old frame. Not only was I pleased, but my daughters begged I make them each one. The requests multiplied. I found myself in production.

My work, though inspired by my valentines, was very different. I seemed to have originated a new way to use an old craft. I decided to call it shell decoupage. These creations were so well received that I suddenly realized here was the answer to my prayer and longing.

I shall not tell you at this point how I work with shells. I'll save that for the end, for it is a gluey and absorbing process and you might easily get firmly stuck right here. Instead I should love to surprise you first, as I have been surprised, by unfolding the many branching avenues of interest, of genuine excitement that have opened up for me along the way: the lore and legend of shells from ancient times; the shell in art and architecture; the astonishing life history of living mollusks.

And this is but a beginning. I must tell you of the happy accidents: spying a rare shell in an unexpected spot, or finding the shell that carries a watch. Often I didn't even have on my glasses—imagine finding Aristotle's lantern without your glasses! Or discovering the elegant Mrs. Delany, a distinguished eighteenth-century artist who raised her shell work to the level of a decorative art worthy of the finest architectural backgrounds. Or the affectionate mother argonaut, creator of the most exquisite cradle on land or sea.

I learned how and where to collect shells I discovered the ways and the haunts of shell collectors. One of the most warming and satisfying results of exploring the treasure world of shells was finding so many new friends, both in and out of books.

There was Aristotle in Will Durant's *Story of Philosophy*. There were Rachel Carson's books, *The Sea Around Us* and *The Edge of the Sea*. There was also Walter Starkie's *Road to Santiago*—when I had finished it I felt almost as though I, too, had made the pilgrimage to Compostela and the shrine of St. James whose emblem is the scallop shell.

Eventually, I joined the shell club which meets on Sunday afternoons at the American Museum of Natural History in New York. Here I met such great shell enthusiasts as Morris Jacobson, who teaches languages and lectures and writes about shells; Anthony d'Attilio, who is an artist in glass design; and also the learned lecturers, Dr. William Clench of Harvard and Dr. R. Tucker Abbott of the Academy of Natural Sciences in Philadelphia. All shared with us, generously and cheerfully, their great knowledge of the sea and its mysterious and varied creatures.

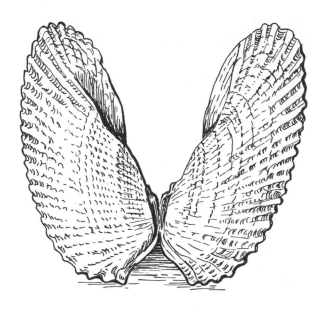

2

The Shellers'
Treasure Island

During these early months of my enthusiasm, I continued making flower arrangements with shells. And here were these little zebras in my candy box. How did these little creatures make those neat, even black lines? With each one, I found myself becoming more and more curious about the shell itself. Like Alice in Wonderland, I would find myself asking them:

> "Come tell me, how it is you live,
> And what it is you do."

About this time Rachel Carson's *The Edge of the Sea*

was published. I had read *The Sea Around Us* and had been wonderfully entertained by her wealth of scientific knowledge, by her imaginative ability to make that little mackerel a real, living person. Her philosophy and the beauty of her prose brought me great contentment as I sat reading on my porch overlooking the water at sunset. The quiet little stream before me, pierced now and then by the playful jump of a small silver fish, had me dreaming and imagining, too. So I hastened to buy her new book with its intimate understanding of my new interest, the shells.

She told about the West Coast of Florida, so it was there I decided I must go.

The delight of having an interest of this sort is that it links us with others who, we suddenly find, have the same interest. My younger sister and her husband were living in Florida. I had long admired his splendid achievements in World War II. As a frogman, he had felt his way under water along the beaches of Iwo Jima to make sure they were free from mines and safe for our Marines to land on and to raise up Old Glory there.

I'm sure he was fond of me as an older sister, but beyond that I could offer him little. However, when I arrived in

Florida with some of my shell pictures to sell, he spotted this and that shell I had used as a petal or a stamen, shells he had found himself in their native, underwater habitat on a Pacific beach. The years that had separated us vanished and we were united in this absorbing common interest.

They insisted on taking me to Sanibel, that West Coast island which is the Mecca of all shell collectors. The trip across the state and the approach to the island on that really picturesque ferry was great fun. Long ago Sanibel was the haunt and delight of Captain Kidd, who is supposed to have buried treasure there. The sea simply leaves its treasure above ground. I would never have believed that one day I would be crunching under my well-soled shoes shells I had been handing out paper money for in the Northern shell shops. It was unbelievable to me.

Here, indeed, the loving hand of the sea has strewn a necklace of jewels on the warm, gentle shore. When you walk these beaches you seldom lift your eyes, the chain of shells becomes so entrancing. Most of them are empty,

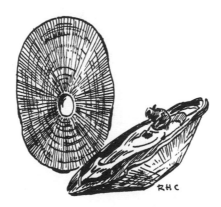

or half shells, vacated by their occupants for various reasons. Storms tear them loose, enemies devour them for food, and so on. But if you find one still housing its builder, you are in for a thrill, for he behaves in surprisingly lively fashion. The animal living within this shell, its architect, is called a mollusk as you probably know, and the study of it is called malacology, which you may not know. The shells themselves are called conches, from the Latin word *concha*, and the exclusive study of them is conchology. At the end of a shelling day, it is hard to decide whether you want to be called a conchologist or a malacologist.

Just one or two days on this West Florida beach opened up a new world for me. The hours are long, for you rush out at the break of day. My experienced companions had noted the time just after the full moon, when the tides are lowest, and you exult if the lowest ebb is at daybreak, for not many will leave their beds that early and you will have long stretches of beach where you are first in this treasure hunt.

You take just one minute for a cup of black coffee. Hours later, when it is time to return to your berth, you can't believe how long you have lasted, how often you have stooped, and how far from your lodging you have wandered. But when the tide comes in again—fortunately, for stamina's sake—you turn homeward for a real breakfast, to kick off your wet shoes and, for me, the chance to put my feet up for a while, exhausted as I am with excitement.

As I rested I thought of Scipio Africanus Minor, the illustrious young Roman general and Consul, aristocrat and scholar, born around 186 B.C. With his friend Laelius, another soldier and intellectual, Scipio and his circle helped to spread Greek culture in Rome. Between campaigns, they were accustomed to visit at the villas of the Roman nobles on the enchanting shore of today's gulf of Gaeta, halfway between Rome and Naples. I had read in a translation from the Latin that "Scipio and Laelius, for the sake of relaxing their minds, used to collect sea shells at Caieta."

Here, no doubt, they found the bright scallop shell and mused on Venus, their goddess of love whose name it bore. These warriors could not dream it would be the symbol of the pilgrims to Santiago and of the Knights of St. James many centuries later. I saw them, not in their battle garb at that time and place, but in their loose comfortable togas. How convenient their sandals would have been for that walk on the beach, and their helmets as receptacles for their finds when they had gathered up more than they could hold. This antique scene became so vivid,† I began to wonder if their toga hems got wet, when the waves took them by surprise, as they stooped to watch a hermit crab sunning in the door of his borrowed home.* Some morning, as I rush from my bed at dawn to be on hand for the lowest tide, I'll wrap myself in a sheet and find out how a toga may have felt on that far distant strand.

On the beach at Sanibel, I first saw the happy, playful scallops. They romp through the waters, gay as young children in their bright colored frocks. I could almost see their jumping ropes! For that is how they move, as they open and shut their pairs of shells, squirting out jets of

---

† I had seen it described in *Sea Treasure, a Guide to Shell Collecting* by Kathleen Yerger Johnstone, The Riverside Press, Cambridge, Mass., 1957.
* This ingenious little fellow is always hunting other creatures' empty shells to back into to protect his fanny, which is soft and hasn't the same protective covering as other crabs.

water which propel them forward a yard or more at a time. They can zigzag, too, if they see danger coming.

If you find their half shells on the sand, you know a scallop bed is near. At low tide we found small ones, the size of a dime, in a shallow puddle—I learned that they do not dig or burrow. When they are partially open, you can see the beautiful color of their mantles, or "lips," and the

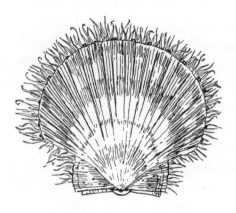

bright row of iridescent eyes in a rim of blue. The starfish, their mortal enemy, can creep up on them so fast that you agonize as you watch the scallop try to escape. Those five arms engulf their pretty prey completely and then open its shell. In the clutches of the starfish, the scallop is completely helpless.

The starfish, I learned, also hunts the unfortunate oyster who cannot even attempt to skip away. During a recent summer, to digress for a moment, two hundred skin divers organized a starfish roundup to save the Long Island oyster farms. A single diver retrieved more than eight thousand starfish, some measuring over ten inches. These big fellows can eat some two dozen oysters in three days.*

At Sanibel, most of the shells you will find on the beach are empty, as I have said. But one day, as the tide went out, the grandchildren and I found a stranded snail-like creature—a common whelk, I learned later. He had pulled his soft body up his winding stair and closed his trapdoor, the operculum, which fits snugly watertight and holds in the moisture that keeps him alive until the next tide comes in to take him out again. This is called intertidal living. When I put him on his back in the wet, he opened his door and reached out and over to the firm sand with his long foot. With this, he gave a great push that turned him right side up. He scuttled off, knowing by instinct which way to go to reach the water.

So the all-too-short days slipped by, and we had to leave Sanibel. On the last morning, my sister noticed young men on the beach shoveling shells into barrels which they loaded onto a truck. We all returned together to the mainland on the same quaint ferry. When she asked them why they were taking back the load of shells, they told her they were selling them to the hotels in Miami.

"And what do they use them for?" she asked, curiously.

"Oh, in the dark of night," they said, "the hotel people

---

* Starfish and men are not the only shellfish lovers. Sea gulls are in on this shell game too. I am reminded of the New Jersey and Long Island coasts where oysters and clams are very plentiful. The highways and bridges connecting these shore areas with the mainland are hard-surfaced and furnish targets for the gulls, who pick up clams as hors-d'oeuvres for their fish dinners. The birds hurl these on the hard roadways, then swoop down to devour the meat from the broken shells. A resident of Rockaway had a new house with a flat roof which the gulls spotted and used as a cracking-ground. The owner was so distracted by the noise that he inquired at the Museum of Natural History and was advised to paint his roof to resemble sea surf and soft sand. That did the trick.

strew them on the beaches for their excited guests to find next morning."

So this, my first trip to Sanibel, had been tremendous fun. But now I had to get back to my workshop, for my novel creations had sold well in Florida—a very great encouragement to me. I was laden with shells I had gathered myself and could hardly wait to put in my pictures. You can imagine how the wheels in my head were spinning! Fired by this experience, I was returning to a cold, wintery city, but there I would have time to read and think and to absorb all the new things in this exciting shell world which I had never before entered nor known I would care so much about.

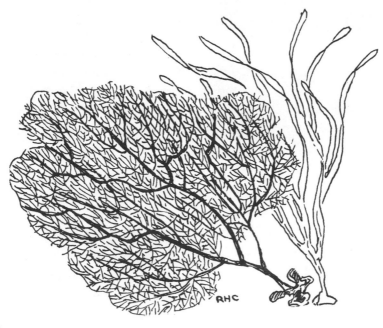

3

In the Beginning...

This glimpse of nature I had had, of the ocean and the creatures living at its edge, made me realize that for millions of years about this earth there had been, here and there, that beautiful merging of land and sea we call the shore. It seems as though the great arm of the ocean embraces the land, his companion. Sometimes it is a gentle, loving and warm embrace; other times it is forceful and tempestuous. Whichever the mood, as his hand withdraws with the ebbing tide he leaves a chaplet of jewels on her breast.

Where she basks in warm sunshine and her skin seems

soft to his touch, his jewels are brilliant and colorful. They are left not singly, but in long chains, to beautify her pale shoulders, white or golden. And where the air is colder and the sands and rocks alter her character, he decks her with some other sort of precious garland, more becoming to her setting there. These shells are Neptune's jewels, the creations of tiny creatures toiling endlessly in the waters among the flora provided in his great ocean depths and in the shallow shore places.

Now I not only wanted to know more about shells; I wanted to go back to their first beginnings, the origins of earth and sea. My youthful learning came back to me— "In the beginning God created the heaven and the earth." The first fact I had to accept was that this earth may be at least five billion years old. As I read, it seemed like a fantastic fairy tale. It was a challenge to try to grasp the thread of narrative that has been spinning since the start of time. I learned, in fact, that there are several theories on how this narrative actually did unfold. One way it is told is that before there were oceans, dense steamy clouds must have enveloped this hot gaseous mass which, it is supposed, had been hurled through outer space from the sun, its parent. At this distance from the sun it went into orbit and after eons of time became our home, the earth. And before the earth's surface cooled and solidified, a great mass or lump seems to have been torn from her side to become the moon; leaving, it may be, that vast hole which is now the bed of our Pacific ocean.

The moon, then, is the child of earth. How happily we behold this child! It not only gives us great joy, it also creates the ebb and flow of the tides. When the moon is crescent and for a few days after, and again when it is full and a few days following, it gives us our greatest extremes in tides—the highest and the lowest. These are the times when collectors enjoy the widest stretch of sands and try to plan their beachcombing for them.

As the outer layer of the earth began to cool, rains fell and continued to fall for years and years, for centuries. When high and low levels developed, "wrinkles" from the shrinking of the earth's crust, the rains filled the lowlands and made our seas. Students of natural science tell us that life, the first living things—not animals or plants but microorganisms—came into being in the waters. These microscopic forms of life, often only one cell, were soft and left no fossil stories in the rocks.

Then as the rains lessened, and the sun shone through more often to warm these first children of the seas, they developed, over the thousands and millions of years, into plants and animals. We know that the algae came first, for animals depend upon plants for their existence. They gradually evolved new cells for specialized functions such as breathing, digesting, reproducing, swimming or taking root. Eventually, these tiny organisms became sponges, corals, worms, barnacles, fishes. Even today it is hard for us amateurs to understand whether a sponge or a coral fan belongs to the plant or the animal kingdom, or to both.

Thus the sea actually prepared life for the dry land,* which was barren and where plants, coming out of the sea, later helped with their roots to pulverize the rock

---

* To quote Jules Verne's Captain Nemo: "The sea . . . it is nothing but love and emotion; it is the 'Living Infinite,' as one of your poets has said." "The globe began with the sea, so to speak, and who knows if it will not end with it? In its supreme tranquility."

into soil and prevent the rains from washing away this new-made earth. These first plants were much like the seaweeds from which they came but, nourished by sun and soil, they grew larger and tougher as time went on.

The earth still had far to go to become man's home, but the long story of creation had begun, and the ocean, the home of the lovely shells, was already sheltering the primitive ancestors of those that would someday wash up on Sanibel's shore.

During subsequent trips to the West Coast of Florida, I spent many happy hours watching, collecting, musing and conversing. Comparing notes with fellow collectors is a popular pastime there. From Rachel Carson I had learned that on this coast is one of the largest mangrove swamps in the world. Mangrove trees first developed and flourished on land, and the present-day mangroves of Florida are a botanical example of that return to the sea which has always baffled scientists. Mangroves, which belong to the highest category of plants, the seed-bearers, probably came to American shores from Africa in seed form, carried here by the Equatorial Current. The individual seedling has a long, pendant shape. It is capable of drifting on current and tide for months, patiently waiting for a solid contact where it can anchor and grow.

Finally, in shallow water, it may meet a ridge of sand, a shell, a piece of decayed wood or a tree root. Instantly it takes hold and begins to grow. Its roots spread out all around, become firmly imbedded in the sea floor, and hold the plant upright against wind and wave. As the roots multiply, they become entangled with the roots of nearby seedlings going through the same process. Into this maze drift all sorts of flotsam—bits of coral, decaying driftwood, sponges and shells. Small sea creatures and vegetation are carried into the strange underwater labyrinth to colonize there; and thus a mangrove island, thousands of islands, develop.

Another kind of tree is made on this same Florida coast by a tiny animal or polyp which, although it may be only one-eighth of an inch long, builds trees taller than a man. Some species, working together in colonies, have built structures a thousand times bigger than man has ever made. This is the coral, the greatest, most versatile architect in the world.*

The Gulf of Mexico and the waters off southern Florida are the only places near the United States where this little animal builds reefs now. In order for him to keep alive and continue to build, the temperature of the water cannot for long remain below 70° F. This coral animal, secreting lime, builds around himself in shapes according to his species.

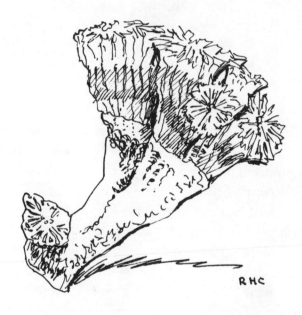

RHC

* Charles Darwin, after he visited the Cocos Islands in the Indian Ocean, wrote of the remarkable coral polyp buildings there: "I am glad we visited these islands: Such formations surely rank high amongst the wonderful objects of the world. We feel surprised when travelers tell us of the vast dimensions of the Pyramids and other great ruins, but how insignificant are the greatest of these when compared to these mountains of stone accumulated by the agency of various minute and tender animals. This is a wonder which does not at first strike the eye of the body, but after reflection the eye of reason."

The living polyp exists only at the outer surface of the structure he is shaping into beautiful and fantastic forms. What he has completed behind the outer cup, with its lime-secreting cells, is his skeleton, as it were. He can paint his house of many mansions, too, since he has the means of producing color. This pigment varies according to his locale and species; it's sometimes gray, sometimes white, or green, or purple; coral color in the Mediterranean; and, in the pipe-organ family of the African coast, a gorgeous deep red.* Like the Smiths and the Joneses, he inherits his color through the genes of his parents, just as some lucky girls are born with red hair because an ancestor had it.

When the corals feed, each polyp opens its protective cup, just as a flower opens its petals. The thousands of stinging cells of the polyps make victims of the microscopic bits of vegetable and animal life that float by. As in all living things, a sort of barter system goes on between plant and animal: the corals make use of the oxygen given off by the plant organisms, and the plants take in carbon dioxide from the corals. It is thus that the coral polyp provides himself with the mortar to build with.

The coral builds not trees alone, but graceful fans and solid mounds in fascinating shapes. The various small-scale *objets d'art* created by these polyps have such descriptive names as "mushroom," "lettuce," "starlet," and "pipe organ." On a far larger scale, however, the Florida Keys (and the Island of Bermuda), coral reefs all and now dry land, were made by these tiny creatures before the last glacial period, which lowered the sea level and exposed them to air and sun. This killed the polyp builders.

---

* In most corals the skeleton is white, but the living polyps are colored; the color is lost when the polyps die.

From an airplane or a glass-bottomed boat, dark patches can be seen today on the reefs of underwater coral, composed of seaweeds, algae, little grasses and the like. All sorts of sea creatures love to make their homes in these patches and among the roots of the mangroves. Here, through a thousand paths and highways they crawl, swim, and court. The animal and plant life of these warm, tropical waters accounts for the fact that the beaches of the West Coast of Florida, and particularly of Sanibel Island, are strewn with so great an abundance of shells.

On this beach you may get your start, although many conchologists have become devoted to their subject without ever having been there. I got my start, really, from the sailors' valentines and that ever so small zebra shell. I must be sentimental and give the credit to them. If you can't get to a beach, hunt up a shell shop near you, or find a mail-order dealer (some are listed at the end of this book). And invest in an illustrated shell book; the shell houses of these ocean creatures are most photogenic. They have evolved these strange and lovely shapes in order best to survive in their particular habitat. Next, then, I want to tell you about some of those special ones whose beauty and personality have captivated or amused me and how I came to know more about them.

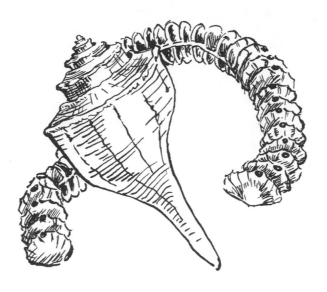

4

Neptune's Jewels

Walking on hard pavements in my unaccustomed city shoes, I went constantly back in thought to that sandy beach in Florida and the fascinating shells I had gathered on it. Their picturesque names I had learned there came easily because they are so appropriate—jingle shells, angel wings, fig, banded tulip, lion's paw, Aristotle's lantern. I had learned that clams are bivalves—they have two shells (Why of course! As bicycles have two wheels!) and uni-valves have one shell—as do snails. I was advancing a bit.

I now had my first big shell book, beautifully colorful, but scientifically beyond me. I needed help and to expose myself to learning more. So, remembering we are never too old, I telephoned the American Museum of Natural History and inquired if any classes in conchology were held there. I learned a shell club sometimes met at the Museum on Sundays. One could qualify for a mere two dollars annual dues, and I did have empty Sunday afternoons to fill. So I joined this really stimulating club. There I met doctors, lawyers, merchants, chiefs, writers, scientists, female skindivers, and artists.

Most picturesque of all was Nick Katsaras, a Greek shoemaker from Bergen County, New Jersey. There he was, reeling off the scientific names, easy for him because of his native tongue. Nick is a collector but he never goes to the beaches and says he does "much better through the mail." He has about three thousand rare and valuable shells and hasn't picked up a single one from the beach. He buys and trades all over the world; his correspondence is fascinating. He can out-trade anyone, and this is easy to understand since he has a winning personality and a contagious enthusiasm. After my first Shell Club meeting he called me Louise. That shows what a common tie will do.

Ten years before, seven intelligent, earnest shell lovers had gotten together to form the New York Shell Club; now its members numbered around two hundred. What a rewarding tribute to the faithful, loyal, and really intelligent seven who have so unselfishly shared their enthusiasm and knowledge.

I suppose I should have felt foolish and embarrassed when I asked one of them where and how the lion's paw got its colors and ridges. But these seven are so patient with beginners that I did not feel uncomfortable when the quiet reply was "oh, the *Pecten nodusus* is a bivalve." I

PLATE 1

PLATE 1

Shell decoupage by the author. The container of this springlike assortment of flowers is a white scallop, family of *Pecten*. Two univalves, Scotch bonnets, serve as feet and the container rests on a base of coral. Berries of the tiny vine hanging over the container are Tahiti tree snails.

The three-petaled white wild roses: white scallops, with small white snails used for centers. The pink roses: pink *Tellina*, commonly called rose petals. The five-petaled blue flowers: common mussels, with small white snails for centers.

In the upper part of the bouquet, the two-petaled white flowers: pairs of *Tagelus gibbus*—a razorlike clam—with yellow money cowries for stamens.

The Queen Anne's lace: tiny clams. The butterflies: coquinas, with sea-urchin spines for antennae.

PLATE 2

An early nineteenth-century sailor's valentine from Barbados.

Left half—Outer border: pink *Tellina* or rose petals. Four turquoise-blue segments: sections of chitons. Four other segments: glossy dove shells. Inner border: pink *Tellina*. Background of center circle: rice *Olivella*. Lettering: tiny *Planaxis*.

Right half—Outer border: alternating segments of pink *Tellina* and common dove shells. Border of the circle: glossy dove shells. Background of circle, and heart: pink *Tellina*. Rose: pink *Tellina* against turquoise-blue background of sections of chitons.

PLATE 3

The Normandy figurines, a bride and groom, *circa* 1800, are probably French, made of shells from the Mediterranean.

The groom's suit: tiny dark mussels. Tiny green pea shells outline the jacket around his ruffly shirt of small white clams. His bouquet and pedestal: assorted small univalves.

The bride's hat: tiny white clams. Her apron: white clams, trimmed with purple fringes of sea-urchin spines. Her skirt: limpets and inverted white clams. Her capelet: sea-urchin spines, trimmed with small univalves. The sleeves: mussels. And the bouquet: white univalves and bivalves.

The angel is also a nineteenth-century figure. The tiered robe is made of the "shells" of the goose barnacle.

PLATE 2

PLATE 3

PLATE 4

Shell decoupage by the author. The basin of this garden piece is a large angel's wing, balanced on a bisque-colored univalve. Above the basin, a sectioned chambered nautilus serves as a sculptured ornament. The single snail on the step at the lower left: *Guildfordia* yoka, the yoka star snail from Japan; this one is in perfect condition.

The clusters of striped scallop shells range from pale pink to dark lavender. The three-petaled white flowers: disc clams, with pointed small white *Terebra* for centers. The four full-blown roses: jingle shells, with striped Cuban tree snails for centers. The large lilylike flowers: fig shells. The brown twisted spirals: the *Vermetu spiratus*, or worm shell.

The purple oval berries on the long vine climbing up at the left: tree snails from Tahiti. The rounder dark grey and pink berries on the short vines: univalves called *Nueritima*. Butterflies: small Atlantic oysters, with sea-urchin spines for antennae.

PLATE 5

Wedgwood shell-decoupage arrangement by the author. The vase is a great scallop supported by a pair of angel's wings. At the center of this base, between the wings: a round-mouthed snail. The single snail at the lower right is a Japanese *Latiaxis* with white coral feelers.

The three-petaled flowers: channeled duck clams, with bleached sea urchins minus their spines for centers. The white roses: various sizes of small clams. Lying flat against the background: round circles of mushroom coral. The spiky twigs are also coral.

Pointed horn shells in the bouquet suggest buds. The lilies of the valley are made of tiny horn shells. The several translucent, very open snail shells are called lady's ear. The butterflies: small coquinas, with feelers of very delicate coral from the Philippines.

PLATE 6

Shell decoupage by the author. The container for this pastel arrangement is the beautiful argonaut. The single snail at the lower left is a *Guildfordia* yoka.

The violet snail at the top of the container: the *Janthina*. Shells with violet rays: the Gaudy *Asaphis*, also called the calico. Conical snails with fine spiraling lines of various colors: Haitian tree snails. The scallop, *Pecten*, in several sizes and colors, makes flat blooms.

The pink roses: *Tellina*, or rose petals. The sprays of small pink flowers: tiny *Tellina*. The stubby white-tipped purple buds on the leafy vines: spines of the Hawaiian sea urchin. Butterflies: coquinas, with cut green-paper antennae.

PLATE 7

This lady's shell work box was made in about 1800, in Minorca. It is still filled with Mediterranean shells. In the deeper spaces hidden by the trays are the larger shells. The small shells are sorted in the sections of the trays.

Under glass in the lid is a basket of shell flowers. These are patterns for shell workers to copy. I have seen these same flowers in other old pieces; the patterns must have been almost standard.

The flowers are made mostly of bivalves. The passion flower so obvious in the top center of the arrangement has small razor clams for petals; its center or Crown of Thorns is a sea urchin.

Plate 8

Shell decoupage by the author. An intriguing Australian oyster, old and rough, serves as container; two pearly polished snails are used for its feet.

The three-petaled flowers, both gray and white: jingle shells, *Anomia simplex*, with polished pearly snails for centers. The two cuplike green blooms: keyhole limpets, *Fissurella barbadensis*, with sea-urchin spines for stamens. The green-patterned snails: *Nerita*. The Queen Anne's lace: tiny white clams.

The lavender butterfly: a bivalve called the *Siliqua*, with sea-urchin spines for antennae and a tiny snail for its head. Sea horses are perched on the paper twigs at the lower right.

was told he eats tiny animals and grasses he finds in the sea. After all this passes through his system, it changes to a substance which will harden as he builds his house to protect his boneless body. This is carbonate of lime, which he uses to build his home instead of making bones as we humans do.

The bivalve's two shells are wonderfully hinged; he can open and shut them at will. His teeth are inside their edges and many have eyes, and of course, he has all the organs necessary for life, plus a very keen sense of smell and hearing in most forms. He also can color his shell. Some are so brilliant, you cannot believe it is true, especially the tropical ones. (Strange, the birds' plumage in that part of the world is so brilliant, too.) And mollusks apparently build faster where the water is warmer. I keep referring to mollusks as "he," but, of course, they are male and female and in some cases both.

The univalve, a word which I roll off easily now, nourishes himself by extending a long tonguelike thing called the radula. On its under side it is covered with tiny teeth, like coarse sandpaper. He sweeps this to and fro, scraping off food from all it passes over.

These creatures build different houses, just as you and I, and what is cleverer than I, they can repair them when they are damaged. They also construct them for the kind of place where they live. I have heard of one around Wainon Bay—on San Christobal Island in the Solomons —a tree snail four inches long, *Placostylus cleryi* Petit, who lives two hundred feet up, and when hurricanes blow the tree down, the dogs and even the natives enjoy him as a rare delicacy. Others must build their houses on rocks, the deep sea bottom, muddy river banks, decayed wood, the sides of wells, or wherever they must live. Up to now I had thought of them as belonging only on sandy beaches.

How interesting their lives became to me, and their original houses. I have caught on to their scientific names by now, though I can't always remember them and have to refer to my notes. Don't be discouraged if you keep forgetting. Shells have their easy names, too, like my first love, the zebra. I sometimes formally refer to him as *Puperita pupa*, but zebra he will always be to me.

Naturally, in working shells into my pictures, I select the most suitable and the most harmonious in color. But in choosing my special pets to tell you of, I am thinking of the live creature and not merely of his shell.

In Florida, among the brightest of Neptune's jewels are the peppermint-striped snails. Highly-colored tree snails are most plentiful in the tropics. It must be wonderful to see them walking the branches with their gay, beautifully marked houses on their backs. As Julia Rogers* writes in *The Shell Book*, it would be "worth a journey around the world" to see. The Cuban savant-patriot, Don Carlos, was an ardent conchologist; his favorite, naturally, was the Cuban tree snail. In 1940 he wrote a monograph on it, and the government did a series of stamps in his honor, using the bright-red tree snail.

Just as fascinating is the 'coon oyster who has learned to live on the roots of mangrove trees. On its shell this mollusk develops four or more little paws that curve and cling to the twigs of the tree. He grows in bunches or

---

* Julia Rogers was born in 1866 and is often referred to in the United States as "the mother of conchology." Dr. Tucker Abbott has been quoted as saying that her book did more than any other single factor to promote interest in shells.

colonies, hanging on the roots of the mangrove like bushel
baskets, mostly above the high-water line. At low tide
raccoons creep down to the water's edge and eat these
oysters with delight. Though they are small, and not often
eaten by man, they make a delicious stew.

Then there is the coat-of-mail, or chiton, which has
eight sections linked together by a rubberlike girdle
which makes him flexible so that he can take the contour
of the rocks he lives on when the surf endangers him. He
clings to them as a suction cup would; the more forceful
the wave that washes him, the tighter he clings. He has
painted, or I should perhaps say finished his interior walls
in the most lovely bluish green. The sections of the coat-
of-mail are often used in the old Barbados valentines. This
fellow harks back to the primitive forms of creation, the
"worms" without shells, or houses, around them. (These
apparent missing links between the worms and the most

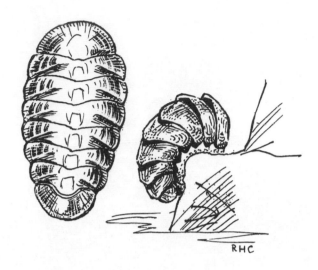

primitive of the mollusks, the monoplacophora, were found only recently, a discovery which set the malacological world aglow with excitement.)

The many varieties of limpets are much like the coat-of-mail in that they, too, have no operculum and cling to the rocks with a sort of suction cup. They move only a few feet from home base throughout their lifetime. When the tide leaves them they go marketing and feed on nourishing tidbits of seaweeds to be found nearby. Several hours later, they return to the very spot they left before the tide comes back to cover it again, just as though they carried watches. Aristotle records observing this.

The pen shell, very common on the Sanibel beaches, spins a golden thread (called "byssus") somewhat like a corn tassel and with this fastens itself to others of its kind or to rocks and corals. This gummy thread hardens when it is exposed to the air. Many centuries ago Mediterranean

36

peoples (Sicilian women, particularly) used to spin this byssus into a fabulously sheer cloth of gold. Another thread spinner, the edible common blue mussel we know so well, secretes a strong network of filaments and fastens onto the piles of docks or bridges. If you look over the edge of a dock or breakwater and down into the water, you will see clinging there hundreds of these mussels which have pulled themselves to the places they want.

The slipper or boat shell is a curious creature which breeds in chains of eight or more; the lowest on each chain are the females. Next above them comes an intermediate sex, and then come the males. As the males age, they become females (what an uncomfortable thought!).

A very clever fellow is called the collector shell, the *Xenophora*, one of the carrier shells. He camouflages himself by fastening onto the roof of his house bits of shell or coral or stone, or whatever he can find nearby. If he should happen to fasten on a half shell, he always does it

RHC

just as the shell falls, concave side up. A complete fooler,
this one! One kind only collects shells on his back; a real
conchologist. Another collects only scraps of rock and
pebbles—a minerologist, you might say. The harp shell,
genus *Harpa*, is lovely in its design. The evenness of the
ridges which, I suppose, are suggestive of harp strings is
amazing. Between these "strings" is a lacy pattern in
white on the beige ground. It is like picoting and as exact
as though a machine had turned it out. Harp shells build in
a most graceful curve. If you decide to be a collector you
must have one of these, but you'll have to shop around, as
you'll not find them on our shores. They inhabit tropical
waters.

The sundial, the *Architectonica*, is also of exact and
symmetrical construction. Its spire rises with the evenness
of stairs, and its pattern of dots on each rise is perfect, too.
It is found in warm waters.

Only a fierce storm or an enemy can loosen from her

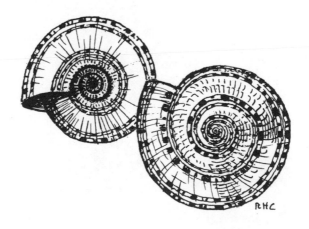

firm foundation the beautiful jewel box which is classed as a rock oyster. The ruffles and flutings on her shell are sheer delight and suggest to me the patterns of peonies or carnations.

And there is the precious wentletrap, one of the most beautifully shaped of all shells. It is a rare shell and comes from the China seas. Circa 1700 it was considered so rare that it brought fantastic prices, selling at up to $200 apiece. Chinese dealers even went to the length of counterfeiting it in a sort of hardened paste concocted from rice. Then the price dropped, but imagine the value of one of the Chinese fakes today!

The cowry is a most interesting shell; some collectors concentrate on it alone. In the past the British Navy had much guardian duty in the Indian and Pacific oceans where many species of these bright shells thrive. In 1844 a Lieutenant Hankey of the Royal Navy took advantage of his shore duty to study them. He became especially interested in the development and growth of the cowry which have long mystified conchologists. Lieutenant Hankey told of having watched the mollusk crack or burst her shell by sheer muscular strength, leaving herself exposed and homeless. His story is not too generally accepted, but he records that she immediately began a new transparent covering, shaped like the other but larger, developing the spire, the narrow doorway and the two lips, and finally painting on her design in enamel. He claims he was unable to collect one for proof of this as the sight was extremely rare and the growing shell so very delicate that it could not be handled.

Cowry shells have been used for money by many primitive peoples and are still a medium of exchange on certain islands in the Pacific. They were accepted currency on the west coast of Africa as late as the mid-nineteenth century. Portuguese traders were interested in cowries as money and called them *porcelanas* because their rounded backs resembled the backs of little pigs.

In 1518, Chinaware—which we call china—was introduced to Europe through the Portuguese, who called this ware *porcelana* perhaps because its hard, glossy surface reminded them of the cowry shell. The French adopted the word *porcelaine* for the fine wares they made at such centers as Limoges, and also called the cowry shells themselves *porcelaines*. There was a popular belief at that time that this ware was made from ground-up cowry shells. The composition of porcelain was long kept secret. William Chaffers in his book, *Marks and Monograms on European and Oriental Pottery and Porcelain*, writes that "Edward Barbosa who died in 1576 says that it was made from marine shells and eggshells buried in the earth for eighty or a hundred years."

The catalogue of Neptune's jewels is nearly endless, and as you can see there is more to their story than the beauty of the shells alone. The life the shell protects is remarkable, too. Another example of this is motherhood in the mollusk world, which is a tender and elaborate business. It surprised me to find how meticulously, in their different ways, these little creatures plan for the blessed event.

On the beach I had often found what I thought were rather dry seaweeds which rattled as I shook them. I broke open one of the pockets of a chain, a yard or more in length, to find it full of the tiniest of snails, barely visible, and in shape the exact replicas of their mother, the whelk.

In the spring of the year, I had also observed a sand formation resembling a tiny horse's collar, perhaps three or four inches in diameter. It is the moon snail that secretes a sort of saliva in the sand and, in her ingenious manner, shapes it in this form. She lays hundreds of tiny eggs under it, completely protected and camouflaged. Watch for these "collars" in the spring.

The violet snail, the *Janthina*, is extremely fragile and beautiful in color. From her little body she excretes a mucus that forms a cellophanelike mattress several inches long. She starts it at birth, and eventually she lays her eggs under it, in neat rows. She clings to it, too. If you are boating off the east coast of Florida, you might see this little bed on the surface of the water and think it is a jelly fish. It is amazing that this delicate shell travels with the purple man-of-war and eats his tissue, so poisonous to others including ourselves. After a storm you may notice the sand tinted lavender where violet snails have been washed up, sometimes with their cellophane nests. You'll find a man-of-war there, too.*

At our New York Shell Club we were told of a certain fresh-water mussel, *Lampsilis ventricosus*, which apparently blows a big bubble, a sort of worm-shaped sac, and fills it with her young. This surprising thing trembles and glistens on the water's surface, attracting inquisitive fish which puncture it. Most of the babes are lost, but some cling to the fish and are nourished by the oil of his skin. He is their wet nurse and is absolutely necessary to their survival. If you are fishing on an inland Florida river in the spring, cut off the fin of the fish and hold it to the light. (The bass is one kind that the mussels can depend on.) The tiny black spots there are these young. The mussel farmer who breeds this mussel for the market knows about this; in the spring he puts these fish into his tanks. He adds the mother mussels who are carrying their eggs at that season. When they expel them, the offspring cling to the fish for dear life until they are able to support themselves. The farmer thus has his supply of mussels safely fattening in his tanks for the epicure's delight.

There is another mother, the *Ampullarius* or apple snail, who, when she finds herself in labor, rushes up the bank and sprays or scatters her eggs in tiny bunches on the grasses. Another one lays her eggs in soft, old wood; they get their strength from it, wiggle around to make the hole more comfortable—much as we do on a pillow—and, with the filelike shells they grow, enlarge it until they are big

---

* Another purple one, but very different, is the *Murex*. It was crushed and used to make a purple dye in the cities of Tyre and Sidon. This was the royal purple which eventually became the prerogative of the Roman emperors.

enough to go out on their own. Both of these you can see in warm inland waters in the spring.

The *Achatina panthera* has a snail-like shape and is one of the agate shells. She makes herself a cottage in charming taste; it looks as though it were made of brown shingles with a raspberry-colored roof. In the soft white sand, she lays one egg almost the size of a robin's.

The most beautiful of all nests is made by an unattractive, many-armed creature suggestive of the octopus. She is called the argonaut, and her nest is sometimes referred to, in error, as the paper nautilus. But she creates a cradle, not a true shell, which does somewhat resemble the shell of the chambered or pearly nautilus.

You must see and hold these delicate things to appreciate them. Aristotle often saw these boatlike objects drifting on the calm sea in the spring of the year but never understood what they were. Being steeped in mythology, he named them *argonauta* after the fabled band of heroes who sailed under Jason in search of the Golden Fleece.

Scientists were for centuries confounded by this frail, empty boat. In 1839 the mystery was solved by a woman scientist who proved that this delicate shell was the egg nest of the soft, many-armed creature that looks like an octopus. Aristotle had already observed the male; he is only one tenth the size of the female, and he has no power to secrete a shell which might attract attention to him. One of his eight arms breaks off when it enters the body of the female. Here it fertilizes the eggs for which the lady argonaut, all her life, has been preparing her cradle. I have never managed to be so bold as to ask a scientist if this little fellow's love life is now ended, whether he grows another

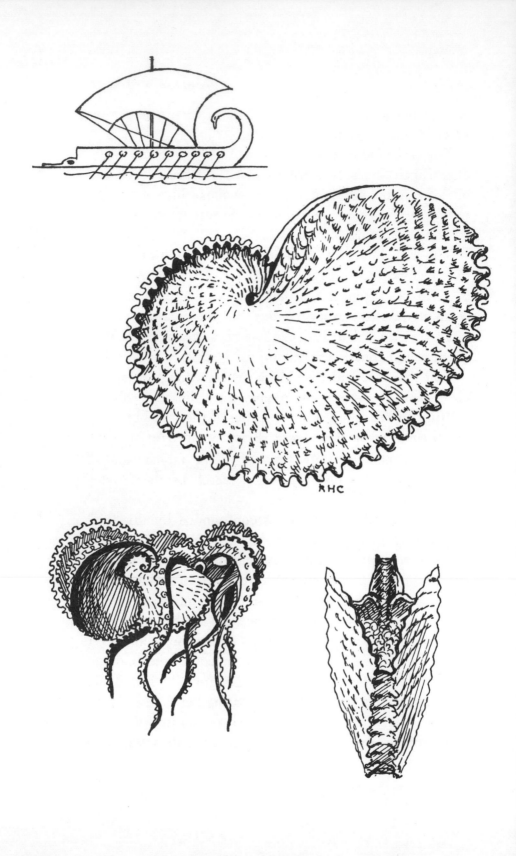

arm, or whether he eventually becomes a basket case.

The argonaut's "shell" is not attached to her body; she holds it firmly and lovingly in two arms, except when she goes into it to lay her eggs. Then, when they are all safely tucked in, she takes it to the surface and sends her babes off alone on their life voyage. Sailors have always considered sighting one of these "a sign of fair weather and favorable winds."

And the argonaut, too, is alone on the open sea. In her *Gift from the Sea*,† Anne Lindbergh has written: "Lovely shell, lovely image—I am tempted to play with it in my mind. . . . Can we middle-aged argonauts . . . look forward to the freedom of the nautilus who has left its shell for the open seas? But what does the open sea hold for us? We cannot believe that the second half of life promises

† Pantheon Books, Inc., N.Y.

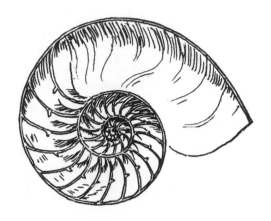

'fair weather and favorable winds.' What golden fleece is there for the middle-aged?"

I have saved for the last what is perhaps my favorite shell of all, the chambered nautilus. He is a cephalopod, like the argonaut, but he is the only member of that family to have retained a true shell. The others, such as the octopuses and squids, have either lost them or have only internal remnants. The nautilus builds his wall around himself, starting this shell with a first room or chamber about one-quarter of an inch around. As he outgrows that chamber, he adds another and then another, each one exactly one-third larger than the one he vacates. When you buy his shell in a shop, it is customarily cut in half so that you can see the great beauty and symmetry of its interior composition.

Each time he outgrows one chamber and builds another,

he carries a siphon through its wall. This siphon's chief purpose is to enable him to fill the chambers of his shell when he wishes to submerge, or to empty them so that they function as air chambers when he wishes to rise to the surface.

In *Twenty Thousand Leagues Under the Sea*, Jules Verne named his imaginary submarine the *Nautilus*, after this creature. (Verne depicts a French scientist aboard who knew shells—and felt when he reached the Island of Crespo just as I did at Sanibel. He writes of this, quoting the scientist: "It was a great grief to me to crush under my feet the brilliant specimens of mollusks which strewed the ground by thousands.")

That was in 1866. Some ninety years later our navy launched its own nautilus, a dream made to come true by the vision of Admiral, then Captain, Rickover. Admiral Kintner ends his account of the trip of the submarine *Nautilus* under the roof of the world with: "The courage, the will, the judgment and resourcefulness which went into . . . the U.S. Submarine *Nautilus*, is an outstanding, successful venture in man's long struggle with nature." I wonder whether those who contributed to this realize that the mollusk whose name they gave their submarine must have had similar resourcefulness to live, as it did, through the physical changes of the earth's surface during the ages that preceded man. For this ingenious mollusk is a descendant of one of the giant animals of prehistoric times, whose fossils of the Jurassic and earlier periods have been found twelve and fifteen feet in size, or more than ten times the nautilus's present size. He had a companion very like him, called the ammonite, which did not survive.

I have a dear little book called *Thoughts on a Pebble; or,*

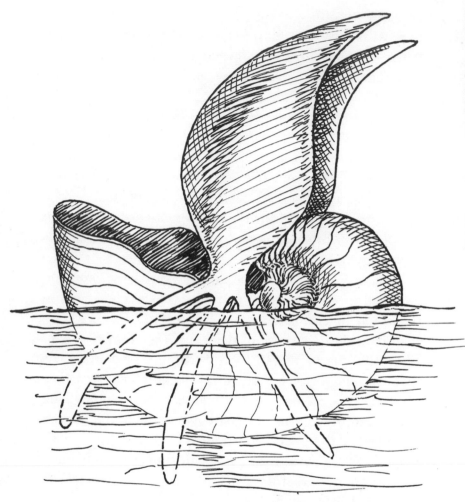

Nautilus from 1849-Wheeler Liquograph

Betsy Mudge

A First Lesson in Geology by Gideon Algernon Mantel, LLD., FRS., vice-president of The Geological Society. It was printed in London and in 1849 was in its eighth edition. I should like to quote part of a poem from this delightful volume because we forget or are perhaps unaware of the friendships animals enjoy.

THE NAUTILUS AND THE AMMONITE
By the late G. F. Richardson, Esq.

The Nautilus and the Ammonite
Were launched in Storm and Strife,
Each sent to float in its tiny boat
On the wide, wide sea of life!

And each could swim on the ocean's brim
And anon, its sails could furl;
And sink to sleep in the great sea deep,
In a palace all of pearl.

And theirs was a bliss more fair than this
That we feel in our colder Time
For they were rife in a tropic life
In a brighter, happier clime.

Thus hand in hand, from strand to strand,
They sailed in mirth and glee,
Those fairy shells with their crystal cells,
Twin creatures of the sea.

But they came at last to a sea long past,
And as they reached its shore,
The Almighty's breath spoke out in death,
And the Ammonite liv'd no more.

And the Nautilus now, in its shelly prow,
As o'er the deep it strays
Still seems to seek, in bay and creek,
Its companion of other days.

I love to put this shell, the nautilus, in my pictures, for I know that whoever has one to see, at the start of the day or in the weariness of the night, will find inspiration in it, a symbol which in its own way has often reminded me of the Psalm: "I will lift up mine eyes unto the hills from whence cometh my help." It was this shell Oliver Wendell Holmes held to his ear and heard a song, as he listened:

> Build thee more stately mansions, O my soul,
> As the swift seasons roll!
> Leave thy low-vaulted past!
> Let each new temple, nobler than the last,
> Shut thee from heaven with a dome more vast,
> Till thou at length art free,
> Leaving thine outgrown shell by life's unresting sea.

The painter, Andrew Wyeth, must have seen something of this same symbolism in the nautilus. I shall not forget that day in a New York gallery when I first saw Wyeth's "Chambered Nautilus." Paintings move each observer differently. It's as though we do not see alike; I sometimes wonder if we do. It is what lies behind the vision of each of us as the image is carried to heart and mind that leaves one viewer indifferent and another moved to tears, "using the eye as the window of the soul."

This canvas of Wyeth's depicts his wife's mother. She is portrayed so tenderly that you feel the painter's fondness for her. She is evidently frail and must spend much time in her lovely old four-poster, with the nautilus close at hand. The bed's canopy and the curtains curve, just as the shell does; and her form follows the same gentle line, as she sits with her back to us looking out the open window.

With the exception of the light from the window, the tones of the picture are in the sepias, the beige and eggshell whites of the nautilus. I believe she must have turned it often in her hands; its contours would have fitted snugly and been a comfort. As she gazed through her window and beyond she, like the shell's tenant, must in spirit have moved on to those higher, vaulted chambers.

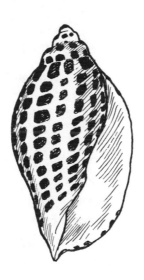

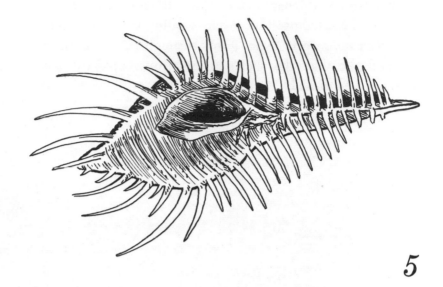

5

The Company of Collectors

I am sure you can understand by now how quickly the conchological bug bites, once you expose yourself to it. Don't feel odd about it, just be glad. Since Aristotle began collecting, men and women have fumbled in the uncharted world of plants and animals, studying and learning and, best of all, enjoying themselves. So may you.

It was reading about Aristotle in Rachel Carson's book that led me to go on to Will Durant's *Story of Philosophy* to find out more about the great philosopher. From Durant's book I learned that Aristotle, who lived in the fourth century B.C., was the first of the Greek philosophers to formulate an orderly approach to the physical sciences. His observations went into textbooks and were considered authoritative for more than two thousand years. The Greeks proved zoology and botany to be sister sciences. Their findings record the mutual dependency of animals and plants, a give-and-take similar to human relationships that sometimes builds up and other times tears down.

As a young man, Alexander the Great was tutored by Aristotle. A close friendship developed. Alexander most probably watched his tutor dissect and study specimens. At any rate, when he became ruler, he gave Aristotle the first zoological and botanical gardens we know of (the equivalent of some four million dollars in state aid), and his soldiers and huntsmen kept these supplied with fauna and flora collected from the length and breadth of his vast empire. (Alexander's interest in sea life, too, was well known. Legend has it that he ordered his glass blower to make a glass barrel, large and roomy, in which he might be sealed and lowered to the ocean floor to observe its inhabitants. A print of a fifteenth-century French artist's conception of this event shows lobsters, fish, mollusks, and even a mermaid gazing back at their visitor. Alexander is supposed to have said: "I have gained much to govern my army more wisely. I have seen in the deep sea many small fish which by their wits baffled their pursuers, a thing which they could not have done by their strength.")

The Greeks' early investigations account for the fact that many shells have Greek names. To this day the internal skeleton of the spiny sea urchin, with its five teeth, so obvious in a live one, is known as Aristotle's lantern. Not only does its shape suggest a lantern, but Aristotle's explanation of its structure and function shed early light on

the mysteries of physiology for science to follow down the centuries.

It was not until the eighteenth century, however, that a truly workable system of classification and nomenclature was devised. Carl Linneaus, the Swedish naturalist, was chiefly responsible for launching the modern, two-name system for identifying plants and animals that is still in use today. It was agreed among scientists that this nomenclature should be based on Latin, a language with which they were all familiar. This cut short the mile-long names used since Aristotle's time, which had described practically everything about a creature—its origin, habitat, and discoverer. Take as an example of the shortened form *Pecten jacobaeus,* the scallop of St. James: The first word now is its genus, or family name; the second, the specific name, comparable to a person's Christian name; and sometimes another is added to designate the discoverer. This simplification was a spur to scientific research in general. It also encouraged amateurs, shell collectors among them. In England it became a fad to collect shells, not only on the beaches at home but also from ships which brought them from every different port around the world. It was at this time that the beautiful wentletrap from China acquired such fantastic value.

Philip Gosse, the nineteenth-century British naturalist, became a great conchologist and collector. His drawings helped and inspired Victorian collectors. He also made possible the fad for home aquaria which entertained the

Victorians, for he understood the complementary exchange that takes place between plants and animals and he was able to establish aquariums with the proper balance of marine plants and animals. Among his writings is a book on sea anemones which is still a classic.*

Charles Kingsley was a great friend and companion of Philip Gosse and often walked the beaches with him. As children, how we loved Kingsley's *Water Babies*! Remember how Tom, the little chimney sweep, was strolling on the beach when he met a professor with an "unpronounceable" name—presumably Gosse—who interested him in not crushing the crunchy things under his feet but in gathering them?

These are but some of the remarkable people of the past you learn about anew when you become a shell collector. You discover you have a special bond with intellectual giants like Aristotle! And the company of shell collectors today is no less varied.

Nowadays, the big colleges have their chairs of malacology, and the museums of natural history strive to perfect their collections and to display them in a way that will interest the general public. The learned men who are responsible for this work are most cordial to amateurs and emphasize the give-and-take between themselves and shell hobbyists. I found this to be true first at the New York Shell Club and again when I attended an annual meeting of the American Malacological Union. We stayed for sev-

---

* If ever you should have the good luck to go bask in the sunshine of the French Riviera, there is a remarkable collection of sea anemones in one of the finest aquariums of modern times at Monaco; I found it much more profitable than the famous casinos. Prince Albert I of Monaco, grandfather of Prince Rainier, made notable deep-sea expeditions and acquired fine marine collections. He established the Institut Océanographique in the late 1880's and completed the aquarium not long after the turn of the century. It is one of the largest in the world and doubtless one of the best peopled as well.

eral days in quarters on the beautiful campus of Haverford College in Pennsylvania. It was August and it was hot, but we rushed from early breakfast to sessions that lasted all day long and were both stimulating and entertaining. Our hosts were Dr. William J. Clench, of the Museum of Comparative Zoology at Harvard, and Dr. R. Tucker Abbott, of Philadelphia's Academy of Natural Sciences. Dr. Joseph Morrison, of the U. S. National Museum, made us amateur collectors feel particularly welcome by remarking that we who love to collect on the beaches can indeed be helpful to the scientists in the laboratories and museums by passing on our finds to them.

There are some remarkable examples of this kind of contribution by amateurs. These are on too grand a scale for all of us to emulate, but I must tell you of one collector, the late Dr. Ramus L. Alsaker of our New York Shell Club, who began collecting as a hobby in 1955. He decided to collect only *Voluta*, aristocrats of the shell world. In five years this collection became so valuable that Dr. Alsaker thought he ought not to keep it in his own house and so presented it to the Smithsonian Institution for the benefit of the public. This, one of the world's greatest private collection of *Voluta*, gives the Smithsonian a boast that very few museums will ever top, and it was done in only five years' time.

The United States National Museum in Washington has acquired a collection of at least five thousand species of shells from the Pacific, Dr. Harald A. Rehder, curator at the Museum, told me. It was a gift from General Alexander Patch who had originally turned it over to the *National Geographic* Magazine on his return to this country after the war. The collection had been, before that, a gift to General Patch from an innkeeper on the island of New Caledonia. This man was so grateful for the arrival of United States troops that he insisted on showing his appreciation by presenting his precious collection of Pacific shells to the general.*

Shell collecting was the absorbing, lifelong interest of William H. Weeks, one of the outstanding collectors of our time, who died in Brooklyn recently, in his eighty-eighth year. Mr. Weeks had lived there quietly all his life in a house on Willoughby Street. He left a shell collection of several million shells of all types. He had corresponded with all the world's leading conchologists and had received shells from them. It seems a little sad that this extraordinary accumulation should be dispersed, but it is exciting for other collectors to know now that Mr. Weeks's shells are being sold by a New York dealer and that you and I can actually acquire some of them.† I have learned of one other collection that is even larger, that of the late Dr. Jeanne Sanderson Schwengel, who was far from an amateur collector, however, having been a serious student and professional researcher and writer associated with important scientific organizations during much of her long life.

These, of course, are very imposing collections. The average collector who takes the matter a little more lightly is still just as fascinated with his hobby. The perfect portrait of the happy amateur appeared some time ago as a cover of *The New Yorker* magazine, by Mary Petty. It showed a well-bred lady obviously just returned to her

---

* This part of the Pacific is a collector's paradise. At Broom, Australia, I am told, the searchers are so avid that the word has had to be passed along that every stone that is lifted must be carefully put back just as it was so as not to harm or disrupt the remaining creatures and plant life.
† See George E. Jacobs, in the list of dealers on page 129.

brownstone house from her summer at the shore. Her tweeds and polished leather oxfords are in the very best British tradition, she hasn't even thought of removing her equally well-bred hat, and her suitcase full of shells stands open as she begins to arrange them on the parlor mantle, quite oblivious to everything else that surely needs to be done. I know just how she feels.

To judge by the number of articles about shells that appear in popular magazines, the general public is tempted by shells, too. The *Reader's Digest* surely reaches a general public, and when it published an article on shell collecting it also showed on its cover, both front and back, many intriguingly beautiful shells in their natural colors. *Sports Illustrated* (of all magazines, along with articles on the Dodgers, horse racing, and golf!) published an article accompanied by twenty color photographs of shells. You never know where the subject will turn up next.

And in a personal way, I have noticed how interested people are. After my first trip to Florida, I continued to carry my shadow boxes of shell arrangements back there during short visits to stay with family and friends. I never needed to seek out a shop to show my shell pictures; a spontaneous word-of-mouth campaign brought the customers to me. You just know that people care about this when they actually want to spend money on it with practically no persuasion at all. One reason is that shells find their place in many other interests that might not at first seem connected. They led me to dabble in science, to read, to meet new people, and to create a new art of my own.

But the place of shells in art is far from new. Once you learn to find them there, it is surprising how far from the collector's beaches your thoughts will range.

6

Shells in
Legend and Art

For two reasons Nick Katsaras decided to have an auction. First, his shells were almost crowding the shoes out of his shop and, second, he wanted to help collectors and encourage collecting. Naturally, I went. The auction, which attracted about seventy-five people, was held in the basement of the National Arts Club on Gramercy Square. The *Turbinella*, a graceful, delicately colored snail-like shell, was put on the block. Anthony d'Attilio, a Shell Club member who was the auctioneer, said, among other things, that this was the sacred shell of the Hindus. Here I was seeing a shell that was a religious symbol and I wanted very

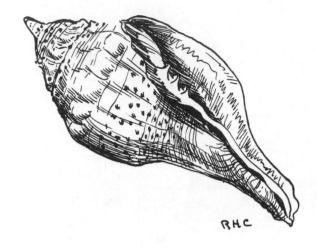

much to have it. Happily, with little difficulty, I got it.

I had been observing, over and over again, that shells as a symbol in religion or legend went hand in hand with shells in art. Shell forms have always captivated painters and sculptors and, as we shall see in the next chapter, architects and designers as well.

The acquisition of the *Turbinella* led me, of course, to seek out the why and wherefore of its sacredness. I learned that the Metropolitan Museum of Art has a twelfth-century stone statue of a Hindu god who is never portrayed without this shell, either in his hand or on his staff. I climbed long flights of stairs and walked what seemed like a mile to find this god. And there he was, the god Vishnu, holding his staff with *Turbinella*. The Hindu, when praying, clasps the shell in his hand believing that his petitions would otherwise not be heard. The priests use it for holding sacred oils. The oil for anointing their

60

princely rulers is kept in the shell from one coronation to the next. Hold one in your clasped hands; it is a most comfortable feeling; also observe that it has a perfect lip for pouring the precious oil. I am sure not a drop would be lost.

I once commented to a friend that I thought a certain shell had been chosen as a Christian symbol, too, but I was vague about it. She told me that when she was in Spain she had made the trip to Compostela, to the pilgrims' shrine of Santiago (Spanish for St. James*) and that his badge was the scallop shell. Immediately, I set out on a quest for more information. Here is what I learned and greatly enjoyed, as I hope you will too.

About 808 A.D., in the northern part of Spain, there was found a small gravestone reading "Here lies Santiago, son of Zebedee and Salome, brother of John, whom Herod beheaded in Jerusalem."

James' mother, Salome (not the dancer, of course), who wished the best for her sons as all mothers do, had asked Jesus if they might "sit, the one on Thy right hand and the other on Thy left, in Thy kingdom." It seems to be established, in more than legend, that shortly after the Crucifixion and Ascension of Christ, His heartbroken followers—especially those who had been closest to Him— traveled abroad to spread His message. Thus, St. James went to Spain to preach the word of Jesus Christ.

According to the legend, St. James made converts and

---

* This was the St. James of the Collect, prayed by thousands on St. James' day in present-day churches, which reads: "Grant, O merciful God that, as Thine holy Apostle St. James, leaving his father and all that he had without delay was obedient unto the calling of Thy Son Jesus Christ, and followed Him; so we, forsaking all worldly and carnal affection, may be ever more ready to follow Thy holy commandments."

established several churches. He returned to Palestine with enthusiasm, one can imagine, to report his success and possibly gather more helpers. However, when he reached there "Herod the king stretched forth his hand to vex certain of the church. And he killed James the brother of John with the sword."

After witnessing his murder, seven of his fellow disciples carried his body to a vessel, according to the legend, to return it to his beloved Spain. An angel, or superhuman being, was their pilot.

One chronicler says that as they sailed up past the shores of Galicia, on the northwestern coast of Spain, a marriage was being celebrated. The bridegroom was on horseback, followed by a colorful procession. Suddenly his horse took fright—unaccustomed, no doubt, to the sight of an angel—and dashed into the sea. When horse and rider rose to the surface, dry and unharmed, they were thickly covered with scallop shells. This miracle was attributed, of course, to the presence of the body of St. James.

The vessel continued up the coast toward the port of Padron which was ruled by a rich lady, by some called Queen Lupa. They begged a burial place for the body of their saint and were refused. Not only that, they were thrown into prison. By another miracle, they escaped and went back to the queen. This time she sent them to fetch a pair of oxen to draw the cart wherein they had placed the body of James. The oxen were actually wild bulls but the disciples tamed them with the sign of the cross and,

having harnessed them to the oxcart, returned once more to Queen Lupa. By this time she was overwhelmed by all these miracles and received them. She became converted, was baptized, and turned her palace into a church.

This, in outline, is one of the legends. And it is not at all clear through the mists of the centuries at what period the scallop was attributed to St. James. There is an early painting by an anonymous Spanish artist in the Prado at Madrid. It depicts two pilgrims accompanying the oxcart in which lies the body of St. James. The scallop shell adorns their hats as well as his. With a fine disregard of the element of time, the artist has painted Queen Lupa, looking down on them from her window, garbed in the elegant fashion of a fifteenth-century lady, certainly not in the dress of 35 A.D. In the background of the painting—again without regard to time, or space—is a boat, presumably the one they arrived in, gently rocking in the harbor and containing the body of St. James who, although beheaded, has the scallop shell squarely sewed onto his hat.

Over the bones of St. James, or Santiago, a great shrine was built, and then the walled city of Compostela rose around it. In the ninth century, the monks of Central Europe had been worried over the wars, particularly the invasions of the Moors from the south who were making a continual battleground of Spain. They reasoned as we do today that if the peoples of the earth knew each other, love and understanding would follow and wars would cease. So the Church decreed that those who traveled to

worship and do penance at this shrine were to be particularly blessed and rewarded for their good works.

The name Compostela means "field of stars" or "way of stars." We are told that the pilgrims trudging westward were to guide themselves in that general direction by the Milky Way. Dante writes in the *Convito* of the galaxy of stars, "the white circle which the common people call the Way of St. James."

As the pilgrims reached Santiago they found that the church authorities had confiscated and controlled the sale of the simple but exquisitely sculptured scallop shell. Each pilgrim bought one and sewed it on his hat or cape as proof that he had made the pilgrimage. The Spanish pilgrims called them *las conchas Santiago;* the French, *coquilles St. Jacques;* we, in English, the shells or cockles of St. James. Just as the Crusaders returning from Jerusalem carried the palm, signifying triumph, so this shell was worn to signify good works and the pilgrimage accomplished.

The scallop as the symbol of St. James does, definitively, appear in paintings and statues of this saint by the thirteenth and fourteenth centuries, not only in Spain, but in churches in France (in a stained glass window in Chartres cathedral dated circa 1200). It was also found in churches in Germany and even in England. When the humble peasant, or even the man in the street, who could not read in those times, saw the scallop on a cathedral's statue he knew it was dedicated to St. James; just as the key or pair of crossed keys told him that a church was dedicated to St. Peter, keeper of the gates of heaven.

This road to Santiago was followed by the humblest and the richest. Popes, bishops, kings, and cardinals rubbed shoulders with priest and peasant. Charlemagne, in the eighth century, was one who followed the Milky Way, as a pilgrim, to worship and do penance at Compostela. Later, he pressed onward to the western coast of Spain, gazed on the vast stretch of the Atlantic Ocean before him, threw his sword in, and declared that further than this no man would go. It is lucky that Columbus had not to lean on him! (And how unlike the great Socrates, who said, "This one thing I know, that is that I know nothing." As you can tell, *The Story of Philosophy* is often on my mind now.)

In the twelfth century multitudes of pilgrims were journeying to Compostela from all over Europe, and the fame of St. James and the scallop was spreading. In the eleventh century in England the pilgrimage was already well known. Throughout the middle ages princes, prelates, and humble folk continued to follow the "Way of St. James." It is said that, at the turn of the fifteenth century, within six months a hundred and twenty-three shiploads set sail from Bristol and other south of England ports for Spain. Many made the journey by crossing the Channel and walking down through France.

Many of these penitent souls gathered in London before setting out at what was called the Hospital of St. James, meaning in those days the Inn of St. James. On this site later rose the Palace of St. James, hence "the Court of St. James's" as we know it today, and St. James Park south of the palace. Those who were unable to follow the pilgrims to Santiago, nevertheless celebrated St. James's day. It is said that it was the custom for the children of London, lacking scallop shells, to pick from the gutters oyster shells discarded by the fishmongers. With these they built small shrines from which to beg alms.

Among the important contributions to medieval art are

the amazing sculptures on the lower portion of the road to Compostela. At Salamanca, to the south and further inland, is the *Palacio de las conchas* whose façade is covered with rows of beautifully carved scallops in a diaper pattern. The shell appears frequently in the stonework of Spanish churches and on their statues. We should use the scallop more often to adorn our own churches, particularly those called St. James.

In 1493, when the pilgrims were flocking to Santiago in great numbers, Ferdinand and Isabella founded the Knights of St. James. The purpose of the order was to protect the pilgrims from attack and to succor them when ill or in need. Their badge was a blood-red sword bearing the cockle shell. There had long been the tradition of St. James appearing in the sky on a great, white charger, routing their enemies, the Moors, on the battlefield. The Spanish rulers wished to invite his continued protection.

Over the years, after Columbus discovered America, the Spanish settlers in the New World remembered their patron saint, Santiago, and his name appears often in South and Latin America. In Mexico, in our time, Diego Rivera has done a great mural with the shell motif predominant.

Again, in recent years, we find Salvador Dali, the Spanish-born surrealist painter, using many shells. In his Madonna de Port Lligat—the town of his birth—Dali has painted the inverted shell over the Virgin's head and from it is suspended the egg, symbol of new life. Shells appear, startlingly lifelike, on the stonework of the columns in the picture and lie here and there on the sand. The *Pholas costata*, the shells which we know as angels' wings and delight to find in pairs, are painted as the wings of Gala, his wife, whom Dali refers to as "the angel of my life"; this painting hangs in the Prado.

The Spanish government commissioned Dali to paint a huge mural for the Spanish exhibition at the Brussels Fair in 1958, and for this he harks back to Santiago, Spain's patron saint. Here St. James is riding his white steed in the heavens over Spain, as they believe he did at the battle of Clavijo, where his presence enabled the Spaniards to turn back sixty thousand Moors and end their shameful yearly tribute of the hundred maidens. The horse's harness is solidly decorated with shells; the architectural framework is riveted with shells; and there is the Milky Way and the weary pilgrim sleeping on the well-worn path. It's thrilling to see it if you know the legend of the scallop, and you will thank Dali for his genius in the portrayal of symbols. (This mural has gone to Fredericton, New Brunswick, in Canada, and hangs in the Fredericton Museum, a gift to the town from Lord Beaverbrook.)

If we look far back before the Christian era, we find the shell used as a symbol in art and also for pure decoration. A terra cotta statue dating from around 400 B.C. depicts a young and lovely Aphrodite kneeling in the scallop shell from which she will soon arise. There are ancient Grecian urns, painted with this same concept, the birth of their goddess of love, showing her head and shoulders as she begins to emerge from between the parted halves of the shell.

Among Renaissance artists this shell was a favorite and was still known as the Venus shell. Everyone is familiar with Botticelli's Birth of Venus, now at the Uffizi in Florence. Titian's Anadyomene is not rising from a shell, but a shell floats on the water where she is bathing.

Another painting, by Piero della Francesca and his asso-

ciates, is a Madonna with saints and angels around her.
The background of the painting depicts a lofty niche with
a scallop shell in its hood from which hangs the egg, the
symbolism Dali has since used. This painting now hangs
in the Brera Gallery at Milan, glowing with the rich reds
and blues of Renaissance color. The niche is supposed to
have been drawn from the porch of an actual church at
Mantua of which Leo Battista Alberti, the Florentine, was
architect.

It was during the late Renaissance, too, that Bernini, the
great sculptor, made his famous Triton fountain in Rome
in which a shell is a main feature. Rome has many fountains
with shells as decoration, for shells, of course, are natural basins, and tilted snail-like shells or conches make perfect spouts.

In the Metropolitan Museum at New York, there is another Renaissance work of art, the jewel chalice by Ben-
venuto Cellini. We climb the main stairway and notice that
a crowd has gathered in the center of the gallery. We find
that they are gazing in wonderment, through a great square

glass case, at this precious *objet d'art*. Sometimes you must wait your turn to find a spot near enough to see its details. Within the glass case is a golden shell, exquisitely chased and adorned with jewels. Its pedestal is an enameled turtle; the handle of the chalice is an enameled mermaid, curved in perfect contour. Its workmanship is unsurpassed. Cellini may have had some symbolism in mind, but to the casual observer this ornament is purely secular, for the time was nearing when shells came to be used more and more as pure decoration.

7

Shells in
Architecture
and Decoration

Sometimes, I might say very often for me, I find it hard to believe that I, one of so many million souls, can possibly contribute to the joy or happiness of the lives around me. I am sure that many people have this feeling; it is not mine alone. And yet, the inspiration to help us overcome it is all around us. It can be found in so many places, or you may find it especially in just one. It is fascinating to consider the contribution to the life of the world that the tiny shell has made when someone with an appreciative heart and mind has stooped to pick it up and hold it in his hand. A beautiful example is the delicate, exquisitely formed

70

temple shell of the Indian Ocean in which the architects of India long ago saw the perfect pattern for their temples.

There is a chapter in the Apocrypha, Ecclesiasticus XLIV, often read in church on All Saints Day, which I love where it begins . . .

"Let us now praise famous men,
  and our fathers that begot us.

"The Lord has wrought great glory by them
  through his great power from the beginning . . .

"Leaders of the people by their counsels
  and by their knowledge of learning
  meet for the people, wise and elegant in their
    instructions . . .

"Such as found out musical tunes
  and recited verse in writing."

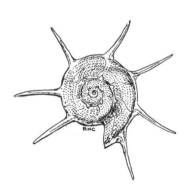

Artists skilled with chisel and brush,
  portraying the lowly shell in stone and color . . .

The last two lines are a topical footnote of my own, for "famous men" have indeed done this. Leonardo da Vinci, for instance, was one of them.

It was during the Renaissance that shells in decoration gradually became secularized. The kings of France and of England invited Italian artists and artisans to their domains and gave them generous patronage. Little by little the lavish baroque style of the Italian craftsmen crept into the design of carved wood and stone of châteaux and palaces further north. Eventually it found its way into architectural ornament in ceilings, mantles, mirrors, and furniture.

In Leonardo da Vinci's time shells and shell motifs were already much in use in Italy in architecture and ornament, and some of the great French châteaux were also decorated with shells, as for example the Château of Blois, near Amboise-sur-Loire, where Leonardo spent his declining years. It is the circular stair which was built there that particularly captures a shell lover's imagination. I happened to pick up my grandson's summer reading one day, Emily Hahn's *Leonardo da Vinci*, written for children; it was just my speed.

Leonardo was born at Vinci near Florence in 1452, the son of a peasant girl and Piero da Vinci, a Florentine notary. Leonardo's contemporaries present a brilliant, breathtaking company—Michelangelo, Botticelli, Raphael, Verrocchio, Galileo, to cite a few. Columbus was born six years before Leonardo, and Andrea Palladio, another great architect, a year before Leonardo died.

Leonardo's father was fairly well-to-do. His son might have had the usual good education, but the boy's inquisitive, imaginative mind led him away from classes when he felt the hills and dales beckoning. Once, as he tells us in his notes, he wandered from school and came across a great layer of rocks with caverns, high up on a windswept hill. He was fascinated and mystified at seeing in these rocks the fossilized forms of leaves, the bones of large fish, and shells. He asked and asked, but no one could explain to him how they got there. He turned this mystery over and over in his head. He gazed long and often on the landscape, observed the low hills, rocks, movement of water, the flowers and trees and the imprints of animals' paws. His earliest drawings are testimony to his sweeping and eager observation of nature. The impression the fossils made on him as a lad ultimately inspired his Deluge series, the depiction of the end of the world, now at Windsor Castle.

When Leonardo was about fifteen his father had him apprenticed to Verrocchio, a Florentine painter and sculptor, who was considered one of the great teachers of his time. Verrocchio, a man of broad interests, taught Leonardo painting and sculpture; he also taught and studied with him mathematics, medicine, astronomy, geology, and other subjects. Leonardo had one of the most versatile minds of all time and grew up to be a man of genius, as you know.

He was constantly making notes, many of which have been lost. For his own amusement—or was it to confuse others?—he wrote his notes backward with his left hand, so that they must be read in a mirror. He could write with either hand. It seems well established that he had a rare wit and sense of humor. No wonder his Mona Lisa smiles!

Some students of Leonardo's life, art and inventions hold that he was primarily left-handed. His contemporaries speak of "the ineffable left hand of Leonardo." He trained himself to use both expertly. The lines in his drawings slant downward from left to right as though done with his left hand. It is said that he did his remarkable anatomical drawings, sketching rapidly with his left hand, while at the same time he dissected his specimen with his more powerful right. Without refrigeration, because of the rate of decomposition, they had to work fast in those days. It almost seemed at times that Leonardo had not only two hands at work but two brains also.

I am specially interested in Leonardo as an architect because he is credited with designing the first circular or spiral staircase. In his notes he tells of conceiving the idea from studying the simple snail shell with its interior spiral whorls. Conchologists say he drew his stair ascending in reverse to that of the mollusk. Hold his drawing before the mirror and it is reflected back exactly like the snail's. There is also a record of a building for which he devised twin spiral stairs, one ascending to the right like the snail's, the other descending to the left. It seems there was no limit to the versatility of this ambidexterous genius.

In my *History of Architecture*, which I now dusted off, Sir Banister Fletcher, speaking of the circular staircase at Blois, says: "The staircase has a beautiful architectural treatment, founded on the medieval corkscrew stair, similar to a spiral shell, and is said to have been designed by Leonardo da Vinci who died at Amboise in 1519." There is no record to prove this, in the case of Blois, but the fact remains that Leonardo's designs for the spiral stair are still in existence.

I say that Leonardo designed the first spiral stair, that is, the first one built in Europe, but perhaps I should modify that by saying that he was the first actually to draft plans for the use of future architects. Hundreds of years before

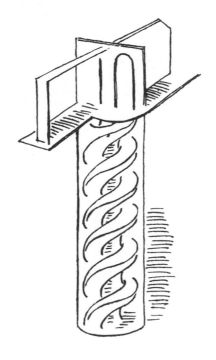

Leonardo's stair, the Spanish Conquistadores had found, at Chichen Itza in Mexico, a Mayan tower with an inner circular stairway. These early builders recognized its similarity to the snail's shell and called it *caracol*, their word for snail. Even today *caracol* is the Spanish word for spiral stair.

Fascinated now with my *History of Architecture*, I was excited to read that the great architects of Greece, around 400 B.C., had found the inspiration for the capital, or volute, of the Ionic column in the perfect growing circle of the interior of the chambered nautilus. Hold two halves of this shell, one facing left and one right, and see how they got the inspiration. They look exactly like the capital. Look this up for yourself lest you think I am inventing it, and then wonder, as they did, how to draw this perfect growing circle without the draftsman's compass we have

75

today. Their answer was another shell—a pointed snail shell, stood upright like a top, with a thread or cord wrapped tightly around the shell's whorls and their type of pencil tied to the end of the cord. As the "top" was slowly unwound, the perfect spirals were drawn.

Returning often now to Fletcher, I found the author telling me how the designers of the Renaissance brought baroque *joie de vivre* into their buildings. In plaster, carved wood, and stone there are garlands, figures, ribbons, and, of course, shells. These are described at times as crimped shells. On one page there are sketches of the shell on a keystone, of another over a dormer window on the Lycée Napoléon in Paris, and on a Louis XV fountain in that same city.

Andrea Palladio was one of these designers. There is a tale that as a youth he worked on a boat, a "join the Navy and see the world" idea, possibly. James Reynolds likes this story and from his book about Palladio* I read: "It has been said by diverse historians and deduced from allusions to letters written by Palladio to friends and patrons in later life, that he shipped on a small sailing vessel borne from Venice to Athens, when he was not yet twenty years old. One point which may be coincidence, but assumed major proportions later, is that the sailing vessel, on which Andrea Palladio was said to have worked his way to Pireas, was loaded with fantastically formed shells from the shores of the Adriatic Sea. These were consigned to a rich merchant whose country house was being completed near Delphi. The shells were to be used to adorn the walls of a grotto in a style then much in favor. A *designa fantastica* for a *grotto di Nettuno*. Later in his life, Palladio used the shell motif in many strange and beautiful forms, as well as the heroic figure of Neptune crowned with sea flowers and branched coral, Trident in hand. . . ." It is within the realm of possibility that the young, enthusiastic, and impressionable artist saw the grotto with its shell-garlanded walls and forever after remembered his youthful reaction to it. At any rate, later, in a book of his own, in a chapter on the work of Vitruvius, Palladio says: "The undulations of the lip of a sea shell may carry out the curve of an arch or intensify the apex of a pediment to fine effect; the bowl of a shell may cradle the head of a ram, an ape, a Bacchus, or any grotesque or monster used as a relief."

Palladio was born a miller's son, in Padua in 1518. He

---

* James Reynolds, *Andrea Palladio and the Winged Device.* Creative Age Press, N.Y.

became one of the greatest architects of the Renaissance and developed a style that for more than four hundred years has influenced building not only in Italy, but in France, England, Ireland, and America. He apparently ran away from home as a boy and was adopted by a stone-carver and mason of Vincenza, who gave him his name. A patron eventually took him to Rome where he studied architecture.

In Rome, Palladio became an ardent devotee of the works of Vitruvius, the great Roman architect of the first century, B.C. Of these days, James Reynolds writes: "We know conclusively, of course, that Palladio journeyed to Rome and was so entranced by the soaring pillars and pediments and ruins of the Caesars that he borrowed measuring gear and spent many hot and steaming weeks through a Roman summer taking exact measurements of these marble monuments to victory and the pagan deities." Palladio apparently did this at considerable risk of life and limb, and he sketched the details of design and recorded calculations of construction for students coming after him.

When Palladio had finished his studies in Rome, he returned to Vicenza where he built the beautiful Basilica and other public buildings. In Venice he built the San Giorgo Maggiore church and several palaces on the Grand Canal. Some of his finest designs are the country villas he built in northern Italy. Palladio was particularly sought after as an architect for homes, one of his real merits being that he made the best of small opportunities and limited materials. The most popular one is the Villa Capra, in Vicenza, also called The Rotunda. This villa has four porticos, each supported by six Ionic columns with their volutes inspired by the chambered nautilus.

England owes much to Palladio.* Colin Campbell, an English architect, in 1723 reproduced this same villa almost exactly for the Honorable John Fane, Mereworth Castle, Kent. This type of plan was similar to that of Stoke Park, Narthants, previously built by Inigo Jones. I am especially entranced by Mereworth Castle because it had a shell grotto which I will tell you about later.

But it was most particularly through Inigo Jones, born in 1573, that England felt the influence of Palladio. When he was sent to Italy to study architecture, he became as ardently devoted to Palladio's style as Palladio had been to that of Vitruvius. Inigo Jones' influence can be seen often in London, and my favorite example of his work featuring the shell is his entrance for the "York Stairs to the River," done in 1626 and "most humbly inscribed to Sir George

---

* As indeed America does also. Our gifted President, Thomas Jefferson, did much to bring the Palladian style to us, as one can see in his beloved Monticello or at the University of Virginia, where the Rotunda, the administration building, is a particularly fine example.

Markham, Bart." At least seven great carved scallop shells are incorporated in its design, and the shell is one of the emblems in Sir George's coat of arms with crest carved in the pediment. The scallop must have had great meaning for this family, though I have not found out exactly why. I am tempted to dream that a devout Markham ancestor sailed down the Thames and to Spain on a pilgrimage to Santiago de Compostela, and that that is why the architect used the *Pecten jacobaeus* so decoratively here. Perhaps that early Markham left from this very embankment, now braced with this handsome stair?

Inigo Jones used the scallop again, inverted, over a circular window in St. Martin's in London and created a stunning big one over a double doorway at Hampstead. At Queens House, Greenwich, Jones did a long room superbly designed in the finest Palladian taste, of which Reynolds says, "The Palladian shell motif decorates the cornice in this room, that becomes a veritable *sala di marina* with all its maritime detail."

As I only get to Italy or Britain via picture books, my pleasure in viewing a building of Palladian influence must be nearer home, in the doorway of a friend's house at Sutton Place in New York City. It is my good fortune to pass through it often, but first I stand a while on the curb and gaze at it. The carved shell over the door is flanked by urns and is as wide as the door itself, the largest man-made one I have seen, and in perfect proportion. Trucks and cars rush by with no eyes to see. When you cross the sill, you can go directly through to the other side of the house and out another door to the garden and see the East River traffic floating by. There is a green lawn and a wall fountain in the shape of another large scallop. What a treat this is

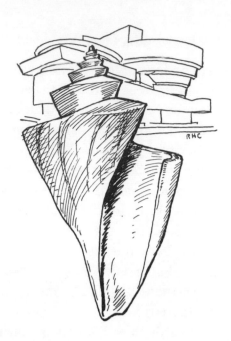

to see, the enduring inspiration of the beautiful shell that has traveled from Palladio's century to ours, from Renaissance Italy to Manhattan.

In our very own time the shell has had its direct influence, too, probably in many instances but surely in one very specific one, the extraordinary and controversial Guggenheim Museum by Frank Lloyd Wright. Mr. Wright said at one time, in the course of a Taliesin Fellowship lecture: "Here, in these shells, we see the housing of the life of the sea. It is the housing of a lower order of life, but it is a housing with exactly what we lack: inspired form. In this collection of houses of hundreds of small beings, who themselves built these houses, we see a quality which we call invention. The beauty of their variation is never finished. It is not a question of principle of design. This multitudinous expression indicates what design can mean. Certainly Divinity is manifest here in these shells in their humble form of life."

82

Shells in Architecture and Decoration

On any scale, grand or modest, the theme of the shell recurs. It is not unusual, for instance, for architects to design architectural accessories and even furniture. They have often worked hand in hand with cabinetmakers, the style and motifs used by the one being naturally an influence on the other, and on other craftsmen besides.

During the rococo period there was almost no limit to the elaborate ornament in furniture. A favorite device was a cabinet or cupboard with a shell-shaped hood like those used over doorways. Countless fantasies including cupids, urns, lyres, griffons, garlands, cornucopias, and shells were the cabinetmakers' delight. This elaboration was sometimes known as *coquillage*, a term that became current in France in about 1740 and came from the word for shell, *coquille*.

As in architecture, there were naturally traces of the shell motif well before this period. Recently there appeared on the market in Paris a very elaborate and rare secretary made in France about 1600. It is inlaid with lapis lazuli and scallop shells in gold leaf.

Sheraton, the famous cabinetmaker, liked the shell motif and signed his pieces with a shell in marquetry. This idea passed on into many unbelievably beautiful marquetry inlays in table tops, tea boxes, and trays. Chippendale adopted shell carvings for tables and chairs. And how perfect these were for the hoods of his secretaries! The scallop shell was especially lovely as a center for a headboard or the top of a mirror frame. The eighteenth-century cabinetmakers also found there was a particular demand they could fill, for special cabinets to house and show the treasures of shell collectors and of the fashionable ladies who had taken up shell work. My sister owns a lovely chest of this period, with many drawers and larger compartments with doors. It is painted in soft yellows and decorated with shells in their natural colors.

Cabinetmakers in Holland took up *coquillage* for their somewhat simpler furniture. One of the more flamboyant French kings ordered a whole set of chairs with the scallop design for the seat. Toussaint-François Foliot, the French *ébéniste*, made chairs in the same design for the shell house at Rambouillet, which I must tell you about a little later.

Designers in the other crafts followed suit. Silversmiths used the shell shape for small trays, bonbon dishes, or flatware—in fact, they still do today. The most enchanting shell designs appeared from the English porcelain factories. Whole tea sets and dinner services were decorated with still lifes of shells, in their natural colors or in golds and greys, softened with decorative strands of seaweeds. These were painted, not printed. In some works the name of the artist of certain shell patterns is still recorded (John Barker for Barr, Flight & Barr). New Hall produced beautiful sets, and my own pride and joy is a simple ironstone plate by Spode. Cake dishes and compotes were made in the shapes of the shells of bivalves and univalves, too.

Mother-of-pearl became fashionable around 1775. Thin sections of it embellished inlaid boxes and trays of *papier-mâché*. Very feminine vanities and sewing tables and even delicate chairs were inlaid. Somewhat later we find pearl-handled tableware, sword handles, and trimmings of all

sorts. The fashion became so well established that the importation of shells for this work was a profitable trade. A firm known as the Shell Transport and Trading Company was one that brought large shipments of shells into England. Later this company went into the oil business and gave up shelling. (Wouldn't we all if we could, at least for a living!) But to this day the descendant of the original company keeps the same name and trademark with which we are all so familiar—The Shell Oil Company and its golden scallop. And if a big business can be said to have a hobby, this one does—the shell in art. Its color advertisements in the magazines are beautiful reproductions of paintings and photographs of *objets d'art*, from many museums, using shell motifs. They are a delight and an artistic education for which not only shell lovers can be grateful.

The very words we use to generalize about styles of design or decoration since the Renaissance have connections

with shells. The French work *rocaille* means rock work or grotto work, which was first popular in France at the time of Catherine de Medici. But artificial grottos also came to be decorated with shells, as we shall see further on, and the word still means elaborate, asymmetrical ornament characterized by the use of shell motifs, among others. For the same kind of decorative style the English borrowed from the French the closely related word rococo; it became an accepted term in the mid-eighteenth century. And the word baroque, which came to be used in the nineteenth century to refer to the same type of thing, also has its clear link with the world of shells, for it is derived from the Italian word *barroco*, meaning an irregularly shaped pearl.*

But now it is of the use of real shells in decoration that there is still so much to tell, and for that we can return briefly all the way to the ancient Greeks.

---

* Captain Nemo, to the question "Sir what is a pearl?":

"My worthy Ned, I answered; to the poet, a pearl is a tear of the sea; to the Orientals it is a drop of dew solidified; to the ladies it is a jewel of an oblong shape, of a brilliancy of mother-of-pearl substance, which they wear on their fingers, their necks or their ears. For the chemist it is a mixture of phosphate and carbonate of lime with a little gelatine; and lastly for naturalists it is simply a morbid secretion of the organ that produces the mother-of-pearl among certain bivalves."

8

Real Shells
in Decoration

The ancient Greeks collected shells to decorate their gardens. The shores of the Aegean and the Adriatic were so rich with shells that they could be used in quantities to line garden pools and fish ponds. How bright and colorful this must have made the water in that sunny clime. The gay little tropical fish must have felt more at home there than they would have in the artificial tile-lined pools of today. This Greek custom, in its natural simplicity, was a distant forerunner of what happened in the gardens of Western Europe during the eighteenth century, when landscape gardening had come into its own.

88

At the peak of the rococo era, real shells for decoration became a vogue which amounted to a rage on both sides of the Channel. They were used especially to make shell houses and grottos in the gardens and parks of great châteaux and houses in France and England.

In 1780, the Duc de Penthièvre engaged the noted painter, Hubert Robert, to landscape Rambouillet Park, his château not far from Versailles.* Several garden pavilions were built and then, for the distraction of the Princesse de Lamballe, he had a small thatched cottage constructed in a romantic setting on an island in the park. His son, the Prince de Lamballe, had been killed in the wars, leaving the young widow inconsolable at Rambouillet. The duke held her in tender affection and wished her to take an interest in this *chaumière* or peasant house. It was here that the princess and Marie Antoinette, her greatest friend, used to meet.

The little house came to be known as the Shell Cottage. On opening the door, one enters a rotunda whose walls and cornices are covered with shells, in patterns delightful in form and color. Spaced around the walls are eight pilasters with Ionic capitals, each one adorned with more than six hundred shells. Between the pilasters are niches crowned with garlands and framing elaborate still lifes of shells. Every kind and color of shell is there—snails of all sizes, periwinkles, mussels, oyster and clam shells, and above all scallops. There is a precious low mantle, faced with shells. What a diversion its building must have been to the sorrowing princess.

The Duc de Penthièvre, who was a patron of

---

* Rambouillet is now the official country residence of the President of France.

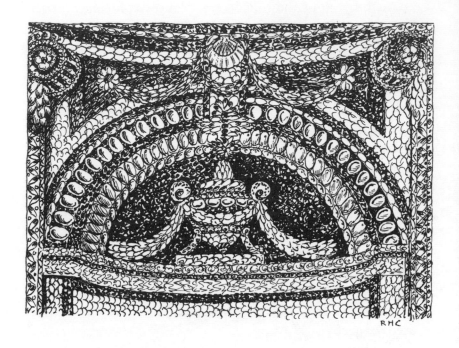

Toussaint-François Foliot, the famous *ébéniste*, asked him to design the furniture for the shell house. Foliot put a straight chair against each pilaster. Their carved seats were shaped like scallop shells, the legs sculptured like branches of coral. He designed four curved love seats painted with shells and pearls in *trompe l'oeil*. In 1794 this furniture was sold at Versailles and later found its way to England. However, in 1941, it was returned to Rambouillet and the shell work in the cottage, damaged by the invading Prussians in 1871, was completely restored. The shell house is once more its beautiful, original self.

In England, women took a hand in creating shell rooms,

entrances from garden to house, and outdoor grottos. Shell grottos became a fashionable and costly adjunct to country houses with their vast parks and woodlands. William Shenstone, a well-known poet, wrote enthusiastically of Lady Fane's grotto. He tells us that it had cost her five thousand pounds, "a sum three times more than her whole house was worth; but it is the most beautiful disposition of shells I've ever seen." We can surmise that he had seen many, for he was also a professional landscape gardener and was, in fact, classed as something of an extremist in landscaping because he advocated the cult of the picturesque. Lady Fane's grotto is still at Mereworth Castle, the Palladian villa in Kent designed by Colin Campbell, and the grotto has been restored. Both are open to the public on certain days of the week.

One of the most famous of shell rooms—and one of the oldest—is at Woburn Abbey, seat of the Dukes of Bedford. This was a precursor of the garden grottos which came into fashion in the eighteenth century. It took ten years to build, was completed in 1640 and is in perfect condition today. It is a dining room, known as Grotto Hall, solidly lined with shells which form designs as in mosaic. There are scenes over the door, and over a small niche with real plants in it, showing figures of cherubs, sea maidens, Neptune, and dolphins.

We have heard much of Woburn Abbey of late since the present Duke of Bedford opened the house and gardens to the public. He tells of caravans of people visiting it, so we may be seeing replicas of Grotto Hall. I think these will have to be family projects, however, labor not being what it once was.

The Duchess of Bedford, incumbent in 1739, must have

enjoyed Grotto Hall, finished some sixty years before her time. There is a record of a great ball given at Woburn Abbey at which the duchess appeared in a gown of "white satin with a mosaic pattern of gold facings, robings and train," with a petticoat of "green paduasoy embroidered very richly with gold and silver and a few colours; the pattern was festoons of shells, coral, cornflowers, and seaweed."

One of the most enchanting shell houses to survive is at Goodwood Park, built in 1780, ancestral estate of the Dukes of Richmond and Gordon. This is entirely women's handiwork. It was executed by the Duchess of Richmond, with her daughters, and it took them seven years to complete. This house, which has a domed ceiling, is solidly covered inside with shells in mosaic patterns, depicting niches with urns containing shell flower arrangements, and the mirrors have shell frames.

Richest of the outdoor shell grottos, perhaps, is at St. Giles in Dorset, built in 1751 by the Earl of Shaftesbury at a cost of ten thousand pounds. All the shells were brought from the Indian Ocean, and many of the oyster shells had pearls still embedded in them. This grotto now is in process of full restoration.

Shell work as a decorative art for the amateur became very fashionable in England, carrying right through into the nineteenth century, especially in projects smaller and less strenuous than shell rooms and grottos. As early as 1703 an impoverished gentlewoman in London advertised in an Edinburgh newspaper that she was prepared to teach shell work in flowers, sconces, and "rocks." In 1782, a Mrs. Hannah Robertson opened a shop in Grosvenor Square to sell materials useful in this craft. She writes that her shop was crowded with the nobility and that she was employed in teaching in the first families in Europe.

George III, who came to the throne in 1760, encouraged handcrafts and founded the Royal Academy of Art. He had his daughter instructed in shell work by her governess, Lady Charlotte Finch, who had studied with Mrs. Robertson. In 1837, when the young Victoria became queen, shell work was still a fashionable hobby. (As queen she visited the famous shell grotto at Carton House in Kildare near Dublin. It was built by the Fitzgeralds in their family home, in the middle of the nineteenth century. House, grotto, and grounds are still in beautiful state today, and they are open to the public at certain times.)

The ladies of the eighteenth century who collected shells or did shell work kept their shells in attractive cabinets specially made for them and appropriately decorated. Merchants around the Mediterranean supplied England with shells and shell work done by the local talent. They made small figures of china or wood, completely dressed with shells and placed under glass domes—collector's items today (see Plate 3). And they made baskets of shell flowers, or garden scenes, and one of the best I have ever seen, a dear old lady at her vegetable stand, each basket filled with shells suggesting cabbages, onions, carrots, or tomatoes.

From Minorca I have a wonderful shell box which I value very highly. It dates from the early or middle eighteenth century. It was found in a great house in Bath with the name of the maker still on it—Miguel Sintes, Plaza del Principe, No. 6 Mahon, Minorca. This island, one of the Balearics, changed hands often among the Moors, the Spanish, the French, and the British but I imagine it could have been an English officer who brought this box home to the object of his affection. Fortunately for me, the recipient evidently did not wish to work with shells, so its contents have not been disturbed. The box is made of rosewood with a simple inlay. It is roughly fourteen by ten inches square and high enough to hold three trays. The trays have delicate wood divisions forming diamond-shaped and circular sections. These hold the sorted shells and their colors in the pattern of the divisions suggest a rose window. On the inside of the lid, behind glass, is a flower arrangement—a model to copy. The arrangement bears the original inscription of the maker, "Floreros de Marisco" which, freely translated, means "Flowers of the Sea." I have seen these flowers, in other arrangements, made in the same way, as though from standard designs. The most fascinating one is the passion flower, its center a small sea urchin with a circle of its spines as stamens, its petals made of razor clams (see Plate 7).

The chief credit for making shell work the popular and fashionable pastime it became goes to two great ladies of the eighteenth century, Mrs. Delany and her close friend, the Duchess of Portland. "The Duchess, Margaret Cavendish-Bentinck, Dowager Duchess of Portland (1714-1785) was for many years the leading patroness of natural history in England, and particularly devoted to conchology," according to a bulletin of the British Museum. "The year following her death, her collection of shells was dispersed at a sale. But some of the shells eventually came to the Museum in diverse ways, including the famous Voluta aulica."

But the claim to fame in the art of shell work and in setting the fashion for design goes first to Mrs. Delany. At the age of thirty-four—and already widowed for ten years —she wrote to her close friend, the duchess, in the language of youth proper for the day: "I've got a new madness! I'm running wild for shells. The beauties of shells are as infinite as of flowers."

When I first began my talks on "Shells through the Ages, in Nature and Art," I actually had less information than enthusiasm for my subject. I was surprised—and delighted—to find how the talks attracted people. The best part of it was that always one or two persons contributed more to my information than I gave them. So it was that I heard about Mrs. Delany, her biography, and correspondence. I knew that I must have this work, but since Mrs. Delany died in 1788 it took quite a search. I finally located one of six volumes, published in 1861, nearly three hundred pages of fascinating letters; I never could have managed five more. I was to enjoy Mrs. Delany because she loved shells; but she loved so much, and so many things beyond the realm of shells, and she so enriched the lives of all women with her handwork and exquisite taste, that I read and reread the book, a little at a time, there is so much to absorb.

Mrs. Delany, nee Mary Granville, in the year 1700, became a painter of note and studied drawing with William Hogarth. She was brilliant, a wit, and a darling in court circles through three reigns, "a great lady of genius in the art of living." Dr. Johnson wrote of her, "I have heard Burke say that Mrs. Delany was the highest bred woman in the world, and the woman of fashion of all ages." We are defeated at birth! She married young and was widowed at the age of twenty-three. Pursued by many, including Dean Swift and Lord Baltimore, she eventually married again, Dean Delany, who took her out of London and carried her off to Delville, his house in Dublin.

There Mrs. Delany continued her painting and also her shell work. She wrote to her friend Lady Hamilton of making a cornice for the ceiling of the chapel at Delville, using "real shells in the manner of modelled stucco." For this project she worked the shells into garlands of flowers which, when finished, resembled fine carving. She also made enchanting shell candelabras for Delville; these were so much admired that she had to repeat them for her sister, Mrs. Dewes at Bulstrode. Mrs. Delany wrote to her sister that she was designing a grotto for the park at the Duchess of Richmond's country house.

A most remarkable achievement in the career of this astonishing woman was her invention of what she called "paper mosaics," begun when she was seventy-four. Mrs. Delany was back in London again, widowed a second time. She sat one day snipping idly with scissors at a scrap of crimson paper, the color of a geranium in her window. She gazed at the flower and kept on cutting. As the bits of paper fell on the table, the Duchess of Richmond came into the room, saw the "petals" falling and asked "Whatever are you doing to the geranium?" Mrs. Delany pieced her paper flower together, pasted it on a black ground, explained it all to the duchess, and a new art was born.

From that day until her eighty-fifth birthday, she went on making her flora, as she also called them. In all, she made a thousand of them, continuing until "my eyes no longer followed the scissors." Horace Walpole praised her new art which drew the admiration, also, of Sir Joshua Reynolds. Sir Joseph Banks, the naturalist, "used to say that he would venture to describe botanically any plant from Mrs. Delany's imitations without fear of committing an error," for they conformed with the originals in every detail of color and shape, down to the last leaf and tendril. The flora are now in the British Museum, except for twenty which Mrs. Delany willed to Queen Charlotte, wife of George III, and which are now in the library at Windsor Castle.

For both her flora and her shell work Mrs. Delany displayed the same delicate artistry and fine taste. She always continued to write to her great friend about their shell work when they could not meet to "pick shells over a cup of tea." It is fortunate for us that these two ladies could not do their visiting on the telephone. If they had, all this prolific exchange of letters between Mrs. Delany and the duchess would have been lost to us, together with the record of Mrs. Delany's role in setting the taste of her times.

Gertrude Jekyll, a landscape gardener of great fame, was born in London in 1843. She was also acknowledged in America and planned gardens here. In some respects she reminds me of Mrs. Delany. She was accomplished in many handcrafts and lived the same long span—even longer—to be ninety. Francis Jekyll, who wrote her biography, I imagine from her diary and many books she herself had written, says: "As her strength and eyesight failed her she was compelled to abandon one after another of her cherished pursuits; only a few shell pictures, whose raised surfaces could be felt rather than seen, served to beguile the long winter evenings." These of course took the shapes of the flowers she had so long known and loved. He continues, "The shell pictures were many of them very elaborate and fanciful creations . . . [and] took the place that paint and canvas had filled in her younger days."

Gertrude Jekyll was far from alone in her craft, as nineteenth-century ladies on both sides of the Atlantic continued to be avid shell workers like their grandmothers before them. They covered anything and everything with shells. Depending on how you feel about the taste of that day, some were very attractive, some were horrors.

The mid-Victorians believed and practiced the adage that woman's work is in the home. I have a faded blue volume, published in New York in 1876, titled: *"Ladies' Fancy Work:* Hints and Helps to Home Taste and Recreations, by Mrs. C. S. Jones and Henry T. Williams, authors of *Household Elegancies."* This has chapters devoted to Paper Flowers, Feather Work, Hair Work, Rustic Pictures—really unbelievable!—and Shells and Ornamental Shell Work. Here readers found recipes for glue and innumerable ideas "to form exquisitely beautiful articles of adornment for parlor or dressing table." It makes most amusing reading.

The Preface to this volume can still be taken to heart by us today: "The subject of Home comforts," it says, "will never have an end. Of all the worthy ways or noble efforts

98

to improve the Home Life of the American people, what more encouraging and appreciative field is there than this of careful, conscientious devotion to the pleasures, recreations and attractions of the Household?

"The little lady of the House, its mistress, longs ever for the delightful moment of each day, when with busy fingers, she can add the useful touches, here and there, which will make the Little Realm more enticing. And if in these few pages which we present, there be found aught that will serve to pass away a useful hour, or suggest a happy hint or device for the ornament of her room, The Authors will feel rewarded as with pleasure they dedicate this bright little volume with its winning pages to THE LADIES OF AMERICA."

One lady of America has made the most attractive display of her shell collection in her Little Realm. She and her husband are tireless collectors; their energy in walking all warm beaches, plus the labor of cleaning and polishing their finds, is amazing. Instead of keeping them filed away out of sight, she has glass-top tables all through her rooms where she arranges them in real compositions. In one table she will make an attractive design of her miniature shells, in another, all her cowries, or scallops, and so on. Her reception room is papered in a graceful Victorian design of ribbons and shells. On one wall, painted shell pink, is a glass case about ten feet long, with glass shelves. On these she arranges her white corals and dried sea grasses with shells scattered through them. These arrangements are most effective because she has a true artistic flair; interesting, too, are her husband's tales of the twelve-foot tides they had to run to escape from after retrieving this or that particularly rare shell. Rearranging, dusting, and adding

99

here and there are his wife's great joy, tasks entrusted to no one else.

With restraint and taste, the latter underlined, you can use shells to decorate your house. Try them with flowers for table decoration. In the spring of the year when lilies of the valley are plentiful, use chalk-white shells with them. Small holders can be placed in the shallow half shell to hold the flowers and their leaves upright. Or, arrange several shells as a center, with corals too, and put the flowers in unobtrusive containers here and there among the shells. In this way, you get an undersea garden, fresh, cool, and green. Tulips will carry out the curves of big conches. Daisies, cornflowers, and Queen Anne's lace with field grasses can be effective and suitable with unpolished shells. And experiment with the flowers and shells you think will best compliment your china and glass.

The highly polished mother-of-pearl interiors of flat bivalves from the Pacific are entrancing for a dressing table. I drop my "pearl" earrings on one as I retire; and then, forgetful, I find them on arising and I think my shell has produced a pearl. These shells are good, too, as ashtrays on porch or terrace, and an upright *Murex* will do well for holding cigarettes.

Shells provide all the colors, and their shadings, that you can possibly need to carry out the décor of any room, be it parlor, bedroom, or bath. I have heard recently of most enterprising uses of shells for baths. In New York a woman, with the help of her maid, has lined and trimmed her entire bathroom with shells. Another in Palm Beach has done the same thing, and *she* went on to have the plumber install a huge white clam shell for a wash basin. It must be lovely!

Naturally, I feel my shell shadow boxes are appropriate for any room in any place—not a pink-and-white arrangement in the library, of course, but grays, perhaps, on a darker background to suggest an etching; or browns with orange and yellow blossoms. I have made delicate, undersea effects to be hung over bathtubs, or a larger, more rustic still life with bamboo frame for a pool house, often with a few sea horses thrown in for luck.

Making these pictures, as I said pages ago, is an absorbing process. Now that I have told you something of the romance of shells, perhaps you will understand better the surprise and delight I have found in working with them—and will want to create pictures of your own with these precious jewels of the sea.

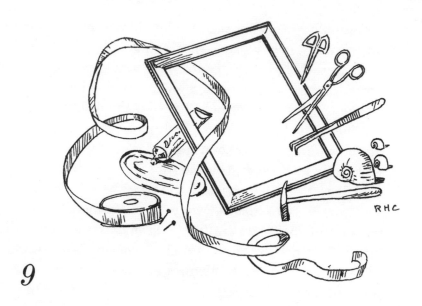

9

Shell Decoupage: How to Do It

I now had a treasure chest full of joys and dreams—dreams for me. The shells I was fondling seemed like petals of a flower, white petals of a tulip, pink petals of a peony. A pair of striped coquinas suggested a butterfly about to alight on one of them.

Once I had had flowers to arrange on table or mantle, this vase or that to fill; but I had them no more, and it seemed these lovely "everlastings" were moving in as if by themselves and forming the very blooms I was missing.

Jules Verne's encouraging statement came to my mind: "what man can imagine, man can do." There was no time to delay or to shop. These "flowers" must be quickly put into a vase. Which vase, and against what background? Necessity—and luck—seemed to spur invention. Before my very eyes a grandchild came playing "lady" in my cast-off chiffon gown. She'd never miss the tag end of the train, I thought—just the heavenly French blue I could not reproduce in paint. A discarded old gilt frame lay on a top shelf—a bit mildewed, perhaps, but all the more interesting for it. The under side of my white desk blotter was clean—the only white background I had, and this is still what I use—so it was easy to trim it to fit the outside edge of the frame (*not* the smaller size of the glass), and then to stretch the chiffon over it, allowing enough to turn back under. I had on hand Du Pont's Duco cement, as essential to my housekeeping as coffee and tea, so I glued the chiffon over the blotter's edge. I placed the old gilt frame over it and was thrilled with the effect. Here was my canvas, prepared and ready. I would have to lay it flat on the table, however, not on an easel, so the shells would not slide off.

Now for a container for my flowers. I had a half of a gray pearly oyster, Pacific, no doubt, in use as an ashtray. The edge was a bit beaten up, but I could trail leaves over that. Its grayness looked well with the mildewed gold of the old frame. And now for the flowers.

I had that old candy box from the rummage sale, full of tropical shells, and masses of small blue mussels and beach clams from the Jersey sands of my summer cottage. These shells I sorted as one would lay out paint on a palette. But what should I use for green leaves? I could not bear to use commercial paint or dye on these shells, so exquisite in their natural colorings. Why not scraps of wallpaper saved from a leafy-papered bedroom? It is great fun to cut out.

Don't hold a roll or big piece of paper, but only a small section that contains what you need. This cutting may seem tedious, but it is also fascinating and quieting, like knitting. Your cuticle scissors must be sharp. Their curve is helpful, of course, as you are going to cut the curves of stems, leaves, and tendrils. You will find you just naturally turn the scissors over when the curve seems to take a new turn. You will also find that you must slant the top blade of the scissors away from the printed side so that the white or under side of the paper won't show. Holding the paper in your hand, you will guide it quite naturally as your scissors clip. You will accumulate a variety of scissors as you progress, and unconsciously you will pick up a different pair for the various kinds of intricate indentation. Also, you may possibly want to change the direction the leaf has taken and reshape it yourself, as a silhouette artist would.* I find it saves time to have an empty stocking box on my lap and let the tiny discarded bits fall into it. Otherwise they jump around and stick in the pile of the carpet and are a nuisance to gather up. The other half of the box will hold the cut-out leaves nicely flat. Throw your tidy collection of bits away, and replace the lid over your paper greens. I used wallpaper for this first try and almost always do; but of course you can find leaves in old books, magazines, catalogues, anything of that sort, once you have the quest on your mind. Sometimes I tint a few of the leaves with water color for a special background.

---

* There is an old art known as "paper work," in vogue about 1750, in which the most intricate tiny pieces of rather stiff white paper are cut and made into all sorts of objects. A swan will have its feathers applied one by one and thus become raised and rounded as its body would be. The delicate leaves of the trees and grasses at the water's edge are most naturally carried out, with a three-dimensional effect. These paper-work pictures, called paper sculpture, are rare now and hard to come by.

Experience has taught me to create my flower, if several shells are going into it, on a separate leaf or round of blotter before putting it on the background. Under this, it is handy to have a heavy piece of glass with beveled edges (if it's not beveled, cover the edges with adhesive or Mystic Tape for safety). This makes a good tray; spilled glue can be easily soaked off its clear surface. Also, if the flower happens to stick a bit, you can dip a paring knife or a palette knife in cold water, and slide it between glass and flower and it will lift off easily. You may have several flowers drying on this tray at once.

In my very first attempt I made the larger flowers of four simple scallops, suggesting perhaps an open tulip or poppy. If you use more shells and smaller ones, they will look like cosmos or daisies. Later you add stamens, as the colors in the stamens may be very important to your design. The pairs of blue mussels found by the hundreds on our East Coast beaches vary so much in size that it is easy to start at the top of a stem with the smallest and graduate them down to the bigger ones and, behold, a delphinium—at least I thought so.

I seem always to feel the need of a butterfly or two. It's not hard to choose which shells to use. All bivalves suggest them. You choose the color and size that fits, and then by luck I thought of the spines of the sea urchins for their feelers. If this winged creature is large enough, a tiny snail will give him a head. I shook with excitement the time a dragon fly grew out of a small razor clam, with a pair of thin iridescent pen shells for wings, a tiny snail for a head, and for the long purple feelers, spines of a sea urchin.

I have a friend who asked, "Louise, with your big hands, how do you ever pick up those tiny things?" I don't. At first I had the tweezers from my dressing table, then I bribed a child for his long tweezers—he had two in his butterfly kit. But best of all, through tears and pain in the dentist's chair, I spied the perfect pair. The dentist was picking up bits of gold to fill a deep hole he had enjoyed drilling, when I said, "I have a great need at home; could I buy your tweezers to fill it?" Sure, he'd order me a pair and also give me his blunt pair. What a break! Look forward to your next appointment with joy and plan to return with loot, for you will see that his tweezers have an angle which makes it very simple to get hold of the thin edge of a shell.

You may say, "I have all before me, but how do I be-begin?" Winston Churchill wrote in his *Painting as a Pastime** of facing his first bare canvas, fearful of the initial step, when his hand seemed "arrested by a silent veto." Then a friendly artist appeared and said to take the biggest brush and begin. "The spell was broken. The sickly inhibitions rolled away. . . . Everyone knows the feelings with which one stands shivering on a spring-board . . . and the ardent glow which thrills you as you emerge breathless from the plunge." I say in the very same vein, "Start gluing." But you can't actually use the glue itself at this stage. Once glued, that's it. So you must first arrange your flowers and leaves tentatively, as you would real ones in an actual vase or container. You will move them here and there. Do you want a fat, solid Victorian arrangement or a simpler, looser affair? The Hogarth line or the Japanese? Or undersea effects may be better for the room in which you plan to hang your work of art.

When you are happy with your design, get out the tube

* Whittlesey House, New York, 1950.

of glue. This is the most precarious part of the procedure. In the hope of saving you from the pitfalls which made me actually cry, and almost drop the whole project, I'll give you some Do's and Don't's from my experience.

First cover yourself with a smock or old dress with very short sleeves (I tear mine out), as your arms and hands are continually passing over these loose objects and sleeves can easily misplace a petal, or several of them.

I happen to love canned shad roe, and the inside of the removed lid is a dandy size on which to rest my open Duco tube. I am very extravagant with the glue, as there is no time to keep replacing the stopper. Also, little gobs of it drop on the tin; it's handy to pull a leaf across one of these, holding the leaf with the tweezers, of course. Or dab a tiny snail in just enough glue to attach him to the background. The reason I say the *inside* of the tin's lid is because the glue will lift the strongest paint off anything it touches and, unless you keep it pure, you'll find you're using red or orange glue just where you cannot hide it. The tin, of course, gets bumpy with unused dried glue hills; but that's no loss. It's time to clean up your table and start a new picture anyway, so you throw it away and eat shad roe again that night. I expect kippered herring would be useful, too—it comes in the same oval-shaped can.

You will work with both hands and all ten fingers. With your left hand, you'll use various tools. Perhaps a cuticle stick, or toothpick, or hairpin, or scissors' point, to help guide the gluey object to the exact spot it must occupy. Your fingers will get full of glue and you can't be bothered with a cloth to wipe it off because, before you know it, the cloth has got itself up on the table and left a gluey spot in the pale blue sky of the picture. So just wipe your hands quickly on your bosom or knees, until, after a few months, your smock is stiff and a work of art itself.

By this time you will realize what a collection of tools and materials you've accumulated. I keep mine on a worthless tray at my right. Besides my various tools I have a bottle of Carbona; I like the smaller bottle. As the tips of the tweezers, and even the scissors and knives, get coated with glue, by letting them hang through the neck of the bottle for a few minutes, I can scrape it off easily. Also, a paint brush and swabs of cotton dipped in this cleaner will remove a slight mark from a shell. Windex, too, is fine to brighten up a shell I may want to use as a highlight. It is also indispensable as a cleaner for the glass of your frame.

Don't ever let anyone talk you into painting your shells. Non-conchologists insist to me constantly that "of course, that bright orange," or "those stripes are not natural," but they just don't know. You don't enjoy dyed flowers when you can have fresh, do you? So, of course not dyed shells.

To quote Max Eastman, "As a practitioner and teacher of the art of perception, that fabulous Bernard Berenson has no equal in history. Indeed, I think his fame as critic and connoisseur is due to the fact that he is not afraid to say that nature can be more beautiful than art. 'As I walk in the garden,' " [Berenson wrote,] " 'I look at the flowers and shrubs and trees and discover in them an exquisiteness of contour, an infinite variety of color, that no artifact I have ever seen can rival.' "

So first arrange your palette. It will come from various boxes of shells, sorted according to species and different sizes and shapes, in the colors you will need for the arrangement you are going to create.

You must plan to start with arrangements that are as shallow as possible, since your frame may have only a quarter-inch or half-inch depth. You will set the glass into the frame and fasten it with tiny brads or nails that will not show later on. After the glass is firmly fastened you will often test the frame's depth over the still unglued arrangement, for a shell may be too high and you must substitute a thinner one which will not reach the glass. You should be sure to do this frequently.

Now you are ready to glue. But you had better walk away from it for a while. Rest your eyes; have a coffee break. Then return for a fresh look and possibly see that one flower turns the wrong way, or note a possibility of improving the composition by adding another bud or leaf, or taking one out.

Now begin gluing. Be calm. Don't get too excited, for you need steady hands; but they will get steadier all the time.

It is not necessary to cover the back of the green leaf edge to edge with glue—in fact, a rather loose effect gives a lighter appearance. Holding the leaf with the tweezers, draw the back of it over a gob of Duco cement, or drop a bit of cement in the center of the leaf. Use the glue sparingly and spread it thin and smooth with palette knife or finger, or else when you press it down to make it stick, too much glue will run out and ruin your background. If this happens, be very quick with a torn edge of blotter and rub like mad. You may be able to absorb it. The other methods I try are too dangerous to print. It is heart-breaking to get glue in the background where you do not want it. Sometimes, as a last resort, you'll just have to put a "butterfly" or "bug" over it, fearful of spoiling your composition. Funnily enough, there are times when I find such an accident improves mine.

Some shells have a sufficiently flat surface so you can fasten them without any trouble. But placing a snail or bivalve in a convex position allows you only the thin outer edge to glue. To get around this, just drop a bit of glue in the concave side, and then put a piece of cotton in there. After the cotton is firmly set, there is more surface to hold the shell to the background. Larger shells need more cotton, of course. The container or vase shell may need a big stuffing, while a slender snail will need thin, pulled bits.

Your finished "canvas" needs a strong backing, so cut a piece of heavy cardboard the same size, and glue it to the white-blotter back securely with a few big swirls of glue. Now place the frame on the picture and turn it over, face down. Tap the back gently with your fingers, so that any shell you forgot to fasten will fall before it is too late.

As I told you, the canvas must be the size of the *outer* edge of the frame, as it needs the depth of the frame to give the shells head room. At first I was very dumb. I fastened the picture to the frame with tiny nails, and the hammering, even though gentle, loosened the shells. More tears. It all had to come apart again. Then wisdom came and I got very small screws, and a small hand auger, or ice pick, to start the holes with. You don't need many screws to hold the picture in place, but you must seal it firmly. There are some dandy plastic tapes you can buy which have "give" to them besides sealing very tight. They are waterproof, too, and join the picture edge over the frame edge beautifully. These tapes come in many colors. You'll use the shade that is least noticeable on the side of your frame. You can cover it after it is on with antiqued gilt paint.

In tidying up your table or tray for the day, be sure to cover your worktable and picture with a light-weight bit of silk or chiffon, to keep off all air-borne particles.

I have no children around, so I need not worry, for my happiest covering is the clear plastic bag from the dry cleaner. I cut them open and they are so light when thrown over the loose objects that nothing moves out of place. Any jolt or accidental brushing would be a catastrophe, for arrangements don't always develop as easily as one could wish and hours of labor could be destroyed in a moment. I have spent as long as a month on a single arrangement before even starting to glue. So plan to work in a place where nothing is ever moved. It is your studio even if it is only ten feet square. Put signs all over it, "Don't Touch," for to lift the covering is a great temptation to all passers-by.

Having done all this, you are still left with your glue-covered nails and fingers. Nail-polish remover is good, but costly, so buy pure acetone in a large bottle and pour a little into your palm, or if your nails are very bad, into a saucer, so you can soak and rub and work off the layers. Do all this carefully as acetone eats into everything it touches. After this, you must cream your hands. Even then, your friends may think you have skin trouble of an unnameable nature, as later you find yourself absent-mindedly peeling off bits of glue—an action which needs explanation.

I had such fun and was so excited over these first creations—and so conscious of their mistakes—that I could hardly wait to tackle another, and another. I acquired a slight improvement in technique each time, developing tricks that made it simpler all the while. And I became more ambitious and strove for three-dimensional effects. You will too, but don't barge into it at first.

This meant that my frame must become a shadow box. I found a cabinetmaker who was so interested in my tale that he gave me scraps of the wood, discarded by his lathe, in varying lengths. My nice building superintendent watched me nervously as I tried to cut them, using a pen-knife. He produced his hacksaw, which I use to this day in constant memory of him.

After resting the glass inside the frame, face down, I then nail in my four pieces of wood, feeling really scared. However, I have only once broken a glass doing this. The inside of these thin wooden walls I then cover with ribbon, velvet or grosgrain. It is difficult to do this neatly. I use a palette knife to spread the glue on the wood, and then quickly press the ribbon over it, smoothing it all the while. There may be an easier way; if you can devise it, tell me, please. On the edge that meets the background, I glue a narrow cord of gilt or silk which gives it a finished look.

Just as in the shallower compositions, you must try your shadow-box frame before gluing to be sure your flowers are not too high. But the depth between the glass and the background of the shadow box now gives you the space to use higher shells and also to make many-petaled flowers. This I finally managed by gluing cotton into the hollow side of bottle caps. With more glue, I set matching shells over the outer edge of the bottle cap; after that row becomes dried and firm, I add the next towards the center, and so on. The white shells suggest a gardenia, and the pink, rose petals, of course—a pink rose. But there is no end to the variety of flowers you can turn out with your variety of shells. You begin to feel like a Burbank.

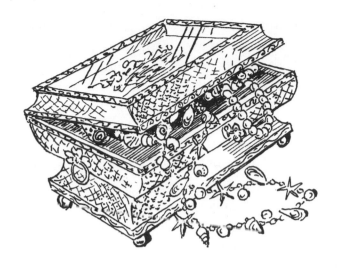

10

A Treasure Chest and a Happy Heart

I decided to call my creations shell decoupage. It seemed to me that it was a decorative art much more akin to the decoupage of eighteenth-century France and England than to the modern art form called collage.

This, as it turned out, was a fortunate choice of words since Dorothy Harrower was writing a book, a fine survey of all kinds of decoupage, and found that my shell pictures fitted into it perfectly. Four of my shadow boxes were reproduced in her book. When my copy of *Decoupage* arrived, I was excited to find my work alongside that of Marie-Antoinette, Lord Byron, and Mrs. Delany!

I was greatly encouraged, also, as I read: "One can easily see the skill with which Mrs. Travers juxtaposes colors, just as in tapestry, where no blending is possible. She is able to bring out color values not observable in themselves, thereby intensifying the illusion of the breadth of her palette."

In the beginning I had made my pictures for·Christmas presents to my daughters. But suddenly I was being offered cash for something that was providing me with satisfaction and sheer joy. The hours were slipping by, a heavy heart becoming lighter. I was astonished, and still am, at the acceptance given my work.

I do become very fond of each picture while I am working on it. I often think *this one* is my favorite, my very best—I can't part with it. But I do, after all. The purchaser is so nice; she wants it for a particular spot, or a special loved one. So I am comforted that it will have a good home and fondly give it a last pat, make note of its new address, and hope that some day I'll be in its neighborhood and pay a call.

At first I remembered who bought them, never thinking the list would grow beyond my memory. So then I got a ten-cent notebook and kept a record. I simply can't believe that I have sent out over one hundred and fifty shell compositions. I mull over these names and picture my shadow boxes in their happy homes.

The first one I sold was then given as a wedding present. I happened to have known the bride's parents and grandparents. So that was nice. I had not thought of signing my shell decoupages, but the bride brought it back to me, insisting that I must consider myself an artist, that no one else should ever claim it. So sign it I did. Presently, there was an invalid who must have one to look at from her couch. Therefore, the first cool, green and white one I made was carried by plane to her home in Hawaii—strange that those shells should return over thousands of miles in so different a context!

A woman in Delray wanted a certain picture I had for a new room in her house there. I said, "That one's not for sale—I love it too much. It would be too expensive." "Well, put a price on it," she insisted. I shot high, as I really did not want to sell it. Quickly she said, "It's sold, and I consider I have a bargain." I nearly collapsed. She intended to decorate her new summer dining room around this big, over-mantle composition with its bronze, peach, and coral tones. The family enjoyed it so much that they insisted upon having another one for winter in their Palm Beach house.

Again, a promising movie star challenged me to do a great mirror frame for her bedroom. This took a different technique, of course; I was branching out and enjoyed doing so, thinking of her talent and her charm as she powdered her nose at my mirror. Our First Lady, as I write this, has one of my early pictures hanging in her bedroom in her house in Virginia.

Another shell picture was carefully carried by plane to Athens and now, lucky thing, hangs in a yacht which is constantly cruising around the Mediterranean. And so it has gone—almost daily surprises for me.

It's fun to make a shell picture for a particular person you love. This tricked me into making a cartoon of a couple walking on the beach with their black dog. Razor clams were wonderful for the man's legs, the worm shell for his cane, tiny blue mussels for his bow tie. Another made a jaunty sun hat. A crab shell, spotted beautifully, was perfect for her freckled face, a bit of seaweed for her red hair. Her short bathing suit had a bouffant blue skirt of mussels. Truly, a shell appeared for each part as I needed it. A shark's egg made their four-legged companion. I don't believe I ever gave a present that was more enthusiastically received.

I really purr, however, when I am shown the handiwork of someone who either saw mine, or bought one, and who tells me I inspired her to try. This is the most gratifying of all. Competition is healthy and, in the art world, very stimulating, for one is a free lance, so to speak, creating one's own style. Just as no two artists paint alike, so you will develop your own genre. You will find the backgrounds you prefer to work on—velvet or chiffon, wood, cardboard, or glass. Follow your own likes and taste. Be a creator.

Another thing I have found is that walking the beaches in search of shells and stooping to pick them up is good healthy exercise. And hunting for old frames is an excuse to stop at every antique shop. Cutting and designing leaves, as I have told you, is almost as relaxing as knitting.

My circle of friends has continued to grow—all these kindred spirits I've found on bookshelves, in the laboratory, on the beach, and at home: there are Aristotle and his discoveries; St. James, the understanding preacher ("Is any among you afflicted? Let him pray; Is any merry? Let him sing Psalms!"); Leonardo, with his childhood interest in fossils and in all creation, his sense of humor in writing his notes backwards; the fascinating young widow, Mrs. Delany (Lord Baltimore bowed low at her final refusal, and she was ill of a fever for some days) who later succumbed to a charming clergyman (I had done the same) and who, also, did shell work. In 1745 she wrote a friend, "To divert my mind from thinking too much of my disappointments, I employ every hour as much as possible. . . . I am going now to arrange my shells to cover two large vases in my garden." Smart woman!

And there were the friendly scientists, so graciously taking time to answer my every question. I think, too, of a professor of music, so understanding with her pet snail "George" whom she has kept alive for three years. He travels in a mason jar. Talk of friendships!

On a hot day Rachel Carson, through her books, takes me again to the cool, green ocean depths; Nick Katsaras, the Greek cobbler, bartering around the world for a rare shell which he brings out of his pocket gingerly, wrapped in toilet tissue, to let me have a peek; and a mystery story writer who works one day a week in a shell shop because its contents and its customers are so interesting to her. And she shares the fun with me.

Kind words always helped me as a girl. "What nice hair you have!" "Your teeth are so white!" And later, "Your husband's so handsome!" "Your girls are so attractive!" No one had been admiring my wrinkles or my waning figure; such flattery had ceased until I began creating and, again, more friends appeared. One of them, searching through old and new bookstores in San Francisco, with me in mind, sends presents constantly to enlighten and encourage me on my way. (She brags: "I have an early Travers!") One purchaser enclosed with the biggest check I had yet received the comment: "I've hung it in my hall; and each time I pass by, I thank God for the talent He has given you."

My friends send me such delightful things, now that they know—and they all do know!—of my new interest. Just as I was finishing this book, a battered envelope appeared in my mail box, from Holland. Inside, safe and sound in spite of its trip, was a reproduction of a tiny Rembrandt etching, dated 1670, of a beautiful single shell, perfect in every detail, and one that I know well, the *Conus marmoreus* Linné, or marbled cone.

I could go on and on: friends, island-vacationing, who carefully pack their finds for me to use; my untiring sisters and grandchildren collecting for me. How I love to think of them as I glue their shells where they belong! I

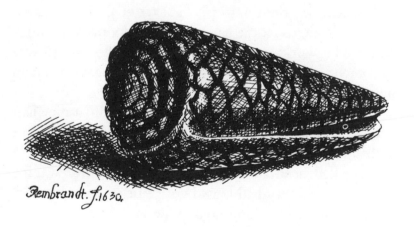

think of one, crippled with arthritis, but stooping and stooping on the sands of Glitter Beach in Jamaica, for those tiny green "peas" I need for flower centers; of an enthusiastic friend saying: "Louise, more people must see your work—it's exquisite!"—and then lending me his large Madison Avenue shop window to display it in.

And especially, now, the dear soul who thinks it's wonderful to have such a happy wife and encourages me to tell this story.

I have opened my Treasure Chest before you. It is a comparatively new possession, but it is filling so fast I'm sure I'll soon need a larger one. The key to it was that first tiny zebra shell I turned over and over in my palm marveling at its creation. How did his stripes come to be so even? Who taught the creature how? Never did I dream this curiosity would lead me to books I'd never opened, into study groups I boldly entered as a complete stranger. These two ventures alone stimulated my mind, dormant since finishing school days. Beaches had always been for bathing only; now they are for high adventure.

On a quiet night, I lift the lid of my Treasure Chest; images rise from it as incense would, filling my heart with joy and companionship. In fact, I must often lock it in order not to be distracted from some pressing mundane task.

The fun I have creating my flower arrangements never wanes. I rush through the morning chores to get to my table when a new-found shell has given me a new idea to play with for color and design. Then I spread my work around me and get just so far when the light begins to fade and my back is tired; only to waken the next day, eager to carry it further.

I look back on these four years or so and realize afresh the "truth of influence"—the pebble dropped in the still pool makes rippling circles ever-enlarging. So the little shell its Creator dropped into my life enriched it beyond belief.

You, too, can hold a shell. Pray do!

SHELL SHOPS
AND DEALERS

The following shops and dealers sell shells by mail and will send catalogues or price lists on request:

SPECIMEN SHELLS FOR COLLECTORS

John Q. Burch
4206 Halldale Avenue
Los Angeles 62, California

J. W. Donovan
3718 Calvin Avenue
West Palm Beach, Florida

F. K. Hadley
48 Adella Avenue
West Newton 65, Massachusetts

Herman W. Hollingworth
Box 355
Seffner, Florida

George E. Jacobs
853 Riverside Drive
New York 32, New York

McArthur Shell Shop
590 Third Avenue
New York 16, New York

George D. Robinson
5347 Dartmouth Avenue North
St. Petersburg, Florida

Sea Gull Shell Shop
1010 Garden Street
Santa Barbara, California

SPECIMEN SHELLS AND SHELLS FOR CRAFTS

Dodson's Shell and Gift Shop
9897 Gulf Boulevard
Treasure Island
St. Petersburg 6, Florida

Florida Marine Museum
P.O. Box 1664
Fort Myers, Florida

Florida Supply House
P.O. Box 847
Bradenton, Florida

Naylor Marine Products
3616 Curlew Street
San Diego 3, California

Neptune's Treasure Chest
Highway 35
Neptune, New Jersey

Newman's Shell Shop
Nags Head
North Carolina

The Shell Factory
P.O. Box 1231
Fort Myers, Florida

Southern Shellcraft Supply, Inc.
P.O. Box 1079
Clearwater, Florida

BIBLIOGRAPHY

I

Without these books I could not have written my own:

Andrea Palladio and the Winged Device, by James Reynolds. Creative Age Press, New York, 1948.

The Edge of the Sea, by Rachel Carson. Houghton Mifflin Co., New York; 2nd ed., 1955.

Gift from the Sea, by Anne Morrow Lindbergh. Pantheon Books, New York, 1955.

A History of Architecture on the Comparative Method, by Sir Banister Fletcher. Charles Scribner's Sons, New York; B. T. Batsford, Ltd., London; 7th ed., 1924.

Ladies' Fancy Work, by Mrs. C. S. Jones and Henry T. Williams. New York, 1876.

Mrs. Delany, at Court and Among the Wits, with an introduction by R. Brimley Johnson. Stanley Paul & Co., Ltd., London, 1925.

The Road to Santiago: Pilgrims of St. James, by Walter Starkie. E. P. Dutton & Co., New York, 1957.

The Shell Book, by Julia E. Rogers (listed below).

The Story of Philosophy, by Will Durant. Simon & Schuster, New York, 1927.

II

Below are a few of the good shell books which may inspire you to become a collector and in which you will find the answers to all the conchological questions an interested amateur is likely to ask:

American Seashells, by R. Tucker Abbott. D. Van Nostrand, New York, 1954.

Caribbean Seashells, by G. L. Warmke and R. Tucker Abbott. Livington Publishing Co., Narberth, Penna., 1961.

Coloured Illustrations of the Shells of Japan, by T. Kira (in Japanese). Hoiknsha Publishers, Osaka, Japan, 1959.

A Field Guide to the Shells of Our Atlantic and Gulf Coasts, by P. A. Morris. Houghton Mifflin Co., Boston, 1951.

A Field Guide to the Shells of the Pacific Coast and Hawaii, by P. A. Morris. Houghton Mifflin Co., Boston, 1952.

How to Know the American Marine Shells, by R. Tucker Abbott. New American Library (Signet Key Book), New York, 1961.

Marine Shells of Tropical West America, by A. M. Keen. Stanford University Press; rev. ed., 1958.

Sea Treasure: A Guide to Shell Collecting, by P. A. Morris. Houghton Mifflin Co., Boston; rcv. ed., 1951.

The Shell Book, by Julia Rogers. Charles T. Branford Co., Boston (1908); rev. ed., 1951.

Shells of the New York City Area, by M. K. Jacobson and W. K. Emerson. Argonaut Press, Larchmont, N. Y., 1961.

INDEX

Operculum of mollusk, 21
Oyster, 20, 'coon, 34-35; rock, 39

Pallidio, Andrea, 76-79
Paper mosaics, 96-97
Paper sculpture, 104n.
Patch, Alexander, 56, 57
Pecten jacobaeus, 54, 81
Pecten nodusus, 32
Pen shell, 36
Penthièvre, Duc de, 89
Peppermint-striped snail, 34
Petty, Mary, 57
Pholas costata, 66
Placostylus cleryi Petit, 33
Porcelain, 45; in shell designs, 84-85
Portland, Duchess of, 94
Puperita pupa, 34

Rambouillet, Shell Cottage at, 84, 89, 90
Razor clam, 105, 115
Reader's Digest, 58
Rehder, Harald A., 56
Rembrandt shell etching, 118
Reynolds, James, quoted, 77, 79
Richardson, G. F., quoted, 49
Richmond, Duchess of, 92, 96
Road to Santiago, 14
Robertson, Hannah, 92, 93
Rock oyster, 39
Rogers, Julia, 34 and n.
Rotunda, 79, 80n.

Sailor's valentine, 11, 12, 13, 30
St. James, scallop of, 54, 61-63, 64, 65, 66; horse's harness decorated with shells, 67, Knights of, 66
San Cristobal Island, 33
Sanibel Island, 17, 19, 20, 21, 22, 26, 30
Scallop, 14, 19, 20, of St. James, 54, 63, 64, 65, 66
Schwengel, Jeanne Sanderson, 57
Scipio Africanus Minor, 18, 19
Sea anemone, 55 and n.
Sea Around Us, The 14, 16
Sea gull, 21n.

Sea Treasure, a Guide to Shell Collecting, 19n.
Sea urchin, 105
Shadow boxes, 101, 112, 113
Shell Book, The, 34
Shell box, from Minorca, 93, 94
Shell Club, New York, 32, 42, 55, 56
Shell Cottage, at Rambouillet, 84, 89, 90
Shell decoupage, 13, 102-12, 113 ff.
Shell grotto, 86, 91, 92
Shell house, at Goodwood Park, 92
Shell Oil Company, shell motif in advertising by, 85-86
Shell Transport and Trading Company, 85
Shell work, 94 ff., 98 ff.; taught by Charlotte Finch, 93; taught by Hannah Robertson, 92, 93
Smithsonian Institution, 56
Snail, apple, 42; moon, 41; peppermint-striped, 34; tree, 34; violet, 41-42
Spiral staircase, suggested by snail shell, 74-75
Sports Illustrated, 58
Starfish, 20-21
Starkie, Walter, 14
Story of Philosophy, 14, 52, 65
Sundial, 38

Temple shell, 71
Thoughts on a Pebble . . . , 47-48
Tree snail, 34
Triton fountain, shell feature of, 68
Turbinella, 59, 60
Twenty Thousand Leagues Under the Sea, 47

United States National Museum, 56
Univalve, 31, 33
Urchin, sea, 105

Venus shell, 19, 67
Verne, Jules, 26n., 47, 102
Villa Capra, 79
Vinci, Leonardo da, 72-74, 116

127